# TRAILBLAZERS
## IN SCIENCE AND TECHNOLOGY

# Larry Page
# and Sergey Brin

## INFORMATION AT YOUR FINGERTIPS

# TRAILBLAZERS
## IN SCIENCE AND TECHNOLOGY

# Larry Page and Sergey Brin

## INFORMATION AT YOUR FINGERTIPS

Harry Henderson

**CHELSEA HOUSE**
*An Infobase Learning Company*

**LARRY PAGE AND SERGEY BRIN: Information at Your Fingertips**
Copyright © 2012 by Harry Henderson

Chelsea House
An imprint of Infobase Learning
132 West 31st Street
New York NY 10001

**Library of Congress Cataloging-in-Publication Data**
Henderson, Harry.
    Larry Page and Sergey Brin : information at your fingertips / author, Harry Henderson.
        p. cm.—(Trailblazers in science and technology)
    Includes bibliographical references and index.
    ISBN 978-1-60413-676-0 (alk. paper)
    1. Page, Larry, 1973- —Juvenile literature. 2. Brin, Sergey, 1973- —Juvenile literature. 3. Computer programmers—United States—Biography—Juvenile literature. 4. Telecommunications engineers—United States—Biography—Juvenile literature. 5. Webmasters—United States—Biography—Juvenile literature. 6. Businesspeople—United States—Biography—Juvenile literature. 7. Internet programming—United States—Biography—Juvenile literature. 8. Google—Juvenile literature. 9. Google (Firm)—Juvenile literature. 10. Web search engines—Juvenile literature. I. Title. II. Series.
    QA76.2.A2H45 2012
    005.1092'2—dc23                                        2011032584

Chelsea House books are available at special discounts when purchased in bulk quantities for businesses, associations, institutions, or sales promotions. Please call our Special Sales Department in New York at (212) 967–8800 or (800) 322–8755.

You can find Chelsea House on the World Wide Web at http://www.infobaselearning.com

Text design by Erika K. Arroyo
Composition by Hermitage Publishing Services
Illustrations by Bobbi McCutcheon
Photo research by Suzanne M. Tibor
Cover printed by Yurchak Printing, Landisville, Pa.
Book printed and bound by Yurchak Printing, Landisville, Pa.
Date printed: July 2012
Printed in the United States of America

10 9 8 7 6 5 4 3 2 1

This book is printed on acid-free paper.

For the people who, still unknown to us, are creating the next Google,
full of promise and challenges

# Contents

# Preface

Trailblazers in Science and Technology is a multivolume set of biographies for young adults that profiles 10 individuals or small groups who were "trailblazers" in science—in other words, those who made discoveries that greatly broadened human knowledge and sometimes changed society or saved many lives. In addition to describing those discoveries and their effects, the books explore the qualities that made these people trailblazers, the personal relationships they formed, and the way those relationships interacted with their scientific work.

What does it take to be a trailblazer, in science or any other field of human endeavor?

First, a trailblazer must have imagination: the power to envision a path where others see only expanses of jungle, desert, or swamp. Helen Taussig, Alfred Blalock, and Vivien Thomas imagined an operation that could help children whose condition everyone else thought was hopeless. Louis and Mary Leakey looked at shards of bone embedded in the rocks of an African valley and pictured in them the story of humanity's birth.

Imagination alone will not blaze a trail, however. A trailblazer must also have determination and courage, the will to keep on trudging and swinging a metaphorical machete long after others fall by the wayside. Pierre and Marie Curie stirred their witch's cauldron for day after day in a dirty shed, melting down tons of rock to extract a tiny sample of a strange new element. The women astronomers who assisted Edward Pickering patiently counted and compared white spots on thousands of photographs in order to map the universe.

Because their vision is so different from that of others, trailblazers often are not popular. They may find themselves isolated even from those who are working toward the same goals, as Rosalind Franklin did in her research on DNA. Other researchers may brand them as "outsiders" and therefore ignore their work, as mathematicians did at first with Edward Lorenz's writings on chaos theory because Lorenz's background was in meteorology (weather science), a quite different scientific discipline. Society may regard them as eccentric or worse, as happened to electricity pioneer Nikola Tesla and, to a lesser extent, genome analyst and entrepreneur Craig Venter. This separateness sometimes freed and sometimes hindered these individuals' creative paths.

On the other hand, the relationships that trailblazers do form often sustain them and enrich their work. In addition to supplying emotional and intellectual support, compatible partners of whatever type can build on one another's ideas to achieve insights that neither would have been likely to develop alone. Two married couples described in this set, the Curies and the Leakeys, not only helped each other in their scientific efforts but inspired some of their children to continue their path. Other partnerships, such as the one between Larry Page and Sergey Brin, the computer scientists-turned-entrepreneurs who founded the Internet giant Google, related strictly to business, but they were just as essential to the partners' success.

Even relationships that have an unhealthy side may prove to offer unexpected benefits. Pickering hired women such as Williamina Fleming to be his astronomical "computers" because he could pay them far less than he would have had to give men for the same work. Similarly, Alfred Blalock took advantage of Vivien Thomas's limited work choices as an African American to keep Thomas at his command in the surgical laboratory. At the same time, these instances of exploitation, so typical of the society of the times, gave the "exploited" opportunities that they would not otherwise have had. Thomas would not have contributed to lifesaving surgeries if he had remained a carpenter in Nashville, even though he might have earned more money than he did by working for Blalock. Fleming surely would never have discovered her talent for astronomy if Pickering had kept her as merely his "Scottish maid."

Competitors can form almost as close a relationship as cooperative partners, and like the irritating grain of sand in an oyster's shell that eventually yields a pearl, rivalries can inspire scientific trailblazers to heights of achievement that they might not have attained if they had worked unopposed. Tesla's competition with Thomas Edison to establish a grid of electrical power around U.S. cities stimulated as well as infuriated both men. Venter's announcement that he would produce a readout of humanity's genes sooner than the massive, government-funded Human Genome Project pushed him, as well as his rival, HGP leader Francis Collins, to greater efforts. The French virologist Luc Montagnier was spurred to refine and prove his suspicions about the virus he thought was linked to AIDS because he knew that Robert Gallo, a similar researcher in another country, was close to publishing the same conclusions.

It is our hope that the biographies in the Trailblazers in Science and Technology set will inspire young people not only to discover and nurture the trailblazer within themselves but also to trust their imagination, even when it shows them a path that others say cannot exist, yet at the same time hold it to strict standards of proof. We hope they will form supportive relationships with others who share their vision, yet will also be willing to learn from those they compete with or even dislike. Above all, we hope they will feel the curiosity about the natural world and the determination to unravel its secrets that all trailblazers share.

# Acknowledgments

I would like to thank Frank K. Darmstadt, executive editor, for his help and suggestions, Suzie Tibor for her hard work in researching and rounding up the photographs, and Bobbi McCutcheon for drawing the excellent line art. Additional thanks must go to all for copyediting, designing, laying out, and printing the book.

# Introduction

When the name of a company becomes a verb, that is a sure sign that they have arrived. In *The Google Story,* David Vise and Mark Malseed, speaking as journalists, describe Google's impact on their own field:

> The enormous media attention focused on Google is a function of the search engine's popular appeal, its place in the zeitgeist of the era, and the heavy use reporters and editors make of it in their day-to-day work. To *google* means "to search." That the company's name has become a verb in English, German, and other languages is testament to its pervasive influence on global culture.

For finding just about anything online—stock prices, where and when a film is showing, a review of the latest and greatest tablet computer, news about a favorite band, or the text of a congressional bill or a court decision—the go to service is Google. Whether using a desktop PC, a notebook or tablet, or even a smartphone, we have grown used to being able to google almost anything at any time.

All the numbers that describe Google are staggering. In 2010, U.S. Web users made 14.4 billion Web searches. As of early 2012, Google had 66 percent of the U.S. search engine market, with Microsoft's newly introduced Bing at 15 percent and Yahoo! at 14 percent badly trailing. Google indexes billions of Web pages into a database of about 100 million gigabytes (100 petabytes).

When Larry Page and Sergey Brin started Google in 1998, it was a classic case of inventors who believed they had come up with a "better mousetrap"—or more precisely, a better search engine. It turned out, though, that the power of that engine and the ways in which users came to rely upon it would enable it to become the locomotive for a whole train of information services. The following is just a few things people do with Google every day:

- upload or watch a video on YouTube
- send or receive e-mail with Gmail
- find places or directions with Google Maps
- surf the Web with Google's Chrome browser
- call someone on a cell phone running Google's Android operating system
- use Google Talk as an alternative to conventional phone service
- create "circles" of friends using Google+, Google's answer to Facebook
- use one of Google's advertising programs to promote a Web site

Besides coming up with a superior search engine, Page and Brin's other big achievement has been finding ways to link advertisers and Web users so that ads seem relevant, useful, and not too obtrusive. The result of this synergy of information and advertising has been to make Google one of the largest, most successful Internet companies. In the first quarter of 2012, Google reported revenue of $10.65 billion, up 24 percent from a year earlier and net earnings of $2.89 billion—a remarkable achievement during difficult economic times.

## NEGOTIATING THE FUTURE

Google itself is so fascinating that it sometimes overshadows the personalities of Larry Page and Sergey Brin. Nevertheless, their personal lives as described in this volume of the Trailblazers in Science and Technology set show how the combination of personal decisions and particular opportunities can lead to remarkable results.

There are two other "characters" in this biography. One is Eric Schmidt, an older, experienced entrepreneur, who, coming on board Google as its CEO, provided needed leadership and management skills, resulting in an intimate working relationship between the three men.

The other character is not a human being at all—it is technology itself. In his 2010 book *What Technology Wants*, Kevin Kelly steps back from the fascinating details of technological progress and looks at the deeper relationship between humans and the tools they have created:

> Technology has domesticated us. As fast as we remake our tools, we remake ourselves. We are coevolving with our technology, and so we have become

deeply dependent on it. If all technology—every last knife and spear—were to be removed from this planet, our species would not last more than a few months. We are now symbiotic with technology.

But where is this new world going—a world in which humans have technology embedded in every aspect of their lives (and increasingly, in their very bodies)? Kelly describes how technology makes new things possible, while making some things easier to do and others harder. (Consider how much one can now do with a cell phone but also how one feels if one finds oneself without one for any period of time.) Kelly suggests that the emerging "organism" of technology that he calls the "technium"

> wants what we design it to want and what we try to direct it to do. But in addition to those drives, the technium has its own wants. It wants to sort itself out, to self-assemble into hierarchical levels, just as most large, deeply interconnected systems do. The technium also wants what every living system wants: to perpetuate itself, to keep itself going. And as it grows, those inherent wants are gaining in complexity and force.

Thus the story told in this book is more than a traditional account of how cleverness, hard work, and perhaps luck turned two Stanford graduate students into billionaires. By seeing the vast possibilities hidden in the early World Wide Web, inventor-entrepreneurs such as Page and Brin helped make possible the rapid evolution of a technology that brings unprecedented possibilities for learning, communication, and social networking even as it challenges us to understand its risks, consequences, and perhaps even its agenda.

## PAGE, BRIN, AND THE GOOGLE STORY

Chapter 1 of this Trailblazers volume describes how two very different lives became connected. While both Page and Brin had families with scientific and technical backgrounds, Page grew up in the American Midwest, while Brin's home was in the Soviet Union. After Brin's family emigrated, Sergey got his undergraduate degree at the University of Maryland, and then went to Stanford University to get a Ph.D. There his part-time job as a student guide brought him into contact with Page. The two computer science students argued with one another but soon found they wanted to spend time together.

A fateful decision begins chapter 2: Looking for a research topic for his dissertation, Page decides to study a relatively new but growing phenomenon of the later 1990s: the World Wide Web. With Brin, they developed a search engine that could rank Web sites according to how many other sites linked to them and how they did so.

By chapter 3, word of the new search engine was spreading around the Stanford campus. When the volume of queries crashed the university's Web server, it became clear that Page and Brin would have to move their operation off campus. The site, which they renamed Google, would have to become a business and somehow make enough money to pay for a growing fleet of computers. Learning to navigate the world of venture capitalists and start-ups, Google began to receive serious funding and landed contracts to provide search services for two Web giants, Yahoo and AOL.

Chapter 4 finds Page and Brin facing the next challenge. To reach the next level of revenue, Google would have to find a way to sell advertising online without alienating its growing legions of users. They find that they can leverage the power of their search engine to target ads to users while making it easier for advertisers to purchase ads. During this time Eric Schmidt comes on board as CEO. Then Google has to face an unexpected challenge—how to provide news and bring people together in the wake of the September 11, 2001, attacks.

In chapter 5, Google finds itself expanding from a search engine to a provider of news, communication, and media. Google Maps and Google Earth provided a new view of the world, but, as Google video vans prowled city streets, questions about privacy and the invasion of personal space began to arise. Another very successful product, Gmail, also created controversy when Google scanned e-mail in order to find matching ads.

The theme of chapter 6 is Google's launch as a public corporation. As one might expect from the unconventional Page and Brin, the method chosen for offering Google stock defied the customs and expectations of Wall Street insiders. Nevertheless, the price of Google stock soared, and Page, Brin, Schmidt, and other Googlers became very wealthy.

Chapter 7 describes how Page, Brin, and Schmidt launched new Google initiatives in the later 2000s. By acquiring YouTube and later introducing Google TV, Google established its presence as a major media company. However, in the burgeoning world of social networking, Google stumbled in its early attempts to take on mighty Facebook. Recently it launched a new service, Google+, that is attracting favorable attention.

Throughout the development of Google, Page, Brin, and Schmidt have had to face conflicting perceptions of Google and criticisms of some of its policies and actions. Chapter 8 begins with an account of Google's attempts to help make the world a better place through its Google.org and foundation. However the difficult issue of Internet censorship—and in particular what to do about China's "Great Firewall"—challenged Page and Brin's original goal of making as much information as possible freely available. Another issue in the wake of the War on Terror is what Google should do when the United States or other governments want information about Google users' online activities or perhaps even the texts of their e-mails. Beyond all this comes perhaps the ultimate issue: Is Google too large, too pervasive, and too powerful for the public good?

The conclusion looks at how Google is changing with the appointment of Larry Page as CEO in 2011 and offers a few possible future Google developments. One, which turns out to be personal for Brin, is the use of Google's technology in genetics. There is also a look at how Google may be changing not just how people find information, but how they think.

# Different Lives, Common Dreams

Larry Page and Sergey Brin were born in the early 1970s, separated by half a world and the cold war. Even though Page was born in the American Midwest and Brin in Moscow, they would find they shared scientifically minded families, a love of technology, and even a special kind of schooling.

## FROM HAMMER TO KEYBOARD

Larry Page was born on March 26, 1973, in Lansing, Michigan. His father, Carl Page, had received a doctorate in *computer science* in 1965, at a time when this field was just beginning to be recognized by universities. He then taught computer science at Michigan State University. After his death the elder Page would be praised by the university as "a pioneer in computer science and artificial intelligence" and "a beloved teacher and mentor to innumerable students."

The Page family's sense of determination and belief in the future went back at least another generation. Carl's father was an automobile assembly line worker. In 1937, he helped organize the strike that forced General Motors to recognize the United Auto Workers union. One day he took Carl and his sister to visit the University of Michigan. Although he had never attended college, he vowed that both his children would go to school there. Larry's maternal grandfather had also been a pioneer labor organizer. He went to Israel and worked as a tool and die maker in the small community of Arad in the harsh desert near the Dead Sea.

1

Larry's mother also held a computer science degree. Although his parents divorced when he was eight, Larry maintained a close relationship with both of them. Larry's father in particular spent a great deal of quality time with the child, including taking him to concerts by the Grateful Dead, an unconventional rock band that has appealed to many creative people.

From 1975 to 1979, Larry attended the Okemos Montessori School (now called Montessori Radomoor). Founded by the Italian doctor Maria

## A COMMON EXPERIENCE: THE MONTESSORI SCHOOLS

Both Larry Page and Sergey Brin attended Montessori schools. Maria Montessori was an Italian physician and educator. She was one of the first women in Italy to receive a medical degree, and she began her career by specializing in what today are called special needs students. At the time, children with cognitive disabilities or behavioral problems were often considered not educable and shunted off into institutions.

Montessori experimented with educational techniques and came to believe that "education is not what the teacher gives, education is a natural process spontaneously carried out by the human individual, and is acquired not by listening to words but by experiences upon the environment."

Montessori's method thus emphasizes creating an environment and activities (such as manipulating blocks, letters, and shapes) that were appropriate for the child's age and that encouraged spontaneous exploration and play. The philosophy behind this is called constructivism and emphasizes children discovering concepts through exploration rather than direct instruction. (The work of Seymour Papert (1928–    ), developer of the Logo computer language, has brought this approach to computer science.)

Montessori learning also has a social dimension. Children are given scaled-down versions of furniture and other items that enable them to set up and run their own small world.

In an interview with Barbara Walters, Page and Brin credited their success to their time in Montessori schools: "We both went to Montessori school, and I think it was part of that training of not following rules and orders and being self-motivated, questioning what's going on in the world, doing things a bit differently."

Montessori (1870–1952), Montessori schools emphasize students pursuing their own interests and learning at their own pace.

# A LOVE OF TECHNOLOGY

Given his parents' background and interests, perhaps it is not surprising that Larry loved technology from the very start. He recalls that his older brother taught him how to take things apart and soon he was taking "everything in his house apart to see how it worked."

According to author Virginia Scott, Page later recalled that while he was growing up with his father his house was "usually a mess, with computers and *Popular Science* magazines all over the place." He also recalled that when he was six he first became fascinated with computers because he got to "play with the stuff lying around." Later, he was the first student in his elementary school to do his homework with the aid of a word processor.

When he was about 12, Larry read a biography of Nikola Tesla (1856–1943). A contemporary of Thomas Edison, Tesla invented a practical system for using alternating current (the kind found in homes today) in generators and motors. Tesla was eccentric (his best friend was apparently a pigeon) but visionary, experimenting and sketching out plans for radio systems and even ways to send power without wires. Larry admired Tesla but took note of his lack of practicality and business sense. Larry would recall that

> . . . from a very early age, I also realized I wanted to invent things. So I became really interested in technology . . . and business . . . probably from when I was 12, I knew I was going to start a company eventually.

Meanwhile, there was the fascination of computers. It would be another decade or more before most kids would have hands-on computer experience, but in *The Google Story* authors David A. Vise and Mark Malseed quote Page's recollection that "We were lucky enough to get our first home computer in 1978. It was huge, and it cost a lot money, and we couldn't afford to eat well after that."

But Larry's interests were not narrowly focused on technology. He was active in the Boy Scouts. In high school he played saxophone in the band—well enough to be chosen for an advanced music camp. Larry also enjoyed reading and arguing about social and political issues—interests that echoed those of two generations of his parents.

## COLLEGE STANDOUT

In 1991, Page graduated from East Lansing High School. As Ken Auletta quotes in *Googled,* his father joked that "We'll pay for any school you want to go to as long as it's Michigan." Thus the younger Page followed in his father's footsteps, going to the University of Michigan to study computer engineering.

Biographers Vise and Malseed quote one of Page's professors as remembering that "Larry just stood out. . . . He was always ahead." His academic performance was matched by the exercise of quiet leadership: He was elected president of the local chapter of Eta Kappa Nu, the computer science honor society.

Page's strengths in computer science were matched by his engineering aptitude. For one project, he needed a printer that could print giant posters. Standard printers could not handle really big sheets, and specialized printers were too expensive. Therefore, Page built his own printer, fitting the electronic and mechanical parts into a chassis made of Lego blocks! (Later, Page and Sergey Brin would make Lego cabinets to hold some of Google's first computer *servers.*)

Page joined LeaderShape, a program designed to encourage talented future entrepreneurs and visionaries. Participants were encouraged to find a practical problem in the world around them and tackle it in unconventional ways. Page focused on the campus's convoluted shuttle bus system. He proceeded to design a monorail system that could link the dorms, classrooms, and other facilities, extending out into the surrounding parts of Ann Arbor. Larry was surprised and disappointed when this futuristic (and expensive) proposal from an undergraduate student went nowhere.

Lack of response to his big ideas did not slow Larry down. It just meant that it was time for the next idea. As he told Steven Levy in *In the Plex,* "Even if you fail at your ambitious thing, it's very hard to fail completely. That's the thing that people don't get." Page would continue to explore alternatives in transportation and energy, helping design a solar-powered car that competed in an international contest. (This interest in solar power would emerge decades later in the form of several Google projects.)

In 1995, Page received his undergraduate engineering degree with honors. He also received the school's first Outstanding Student Award. Meanwhile, in planning for his graduate studies, Page was seriously considering going to Stanford University, which had one of the nation's best computer science programs. (Stanford was also known for pioneering work in artificial intelligence and robotics.) But Page was uncertain whether he would fit into the life of the Stanford campus and the nearby San Francisco Bay Area communities that had become known as Silicon Valley because of their concentration of electronics manufacturing and software companies. He decided to arrange for a tour of the campus and to explore the surrounding area.

Page was impressed by the quality of the research and the facilities at Stanford, and he found he enjoyed the cosmopolitan atmosphere of San Francisco. However he found he was constantly arguing with the student guide who had been assigned to him. Indeed, as quoted in John Battelle's book *The Search,* he thought the guide was "pretty obnoxious." The guide was a bit older and rather outgoing and expansive. His name was Sergey Brin.

## FROM RUSSIA WITH DETERMINATION

The road that brought Sergey Brin to Stanford began in a quite different world from middle class America. Sergey was born on August 21, 1973, in Moscow, the capital of what was then the Soviet Union.

In some respects, the Brin family was similar to the Pages. Sergey's father, Michael, was also a professional—an economist, employed by GOSPLAN, the Soviet central planning agency. His mother, Eugenia, worked in a research lab at the Soviet Oil and Gas Institute.

The Soviet system placed considerable value on scientists and technologists. The Brin family, which also included Sergey's paternal grandmother, had a small apartment to themselves, a bit of a luxury for the professional class when most working class families had to share living quarters.

Michael, however, had wider dreams. He had wanted to be an astronomer. However he was a Jew, and the Soviet government discriminated against Jews. Even though Jews were not supposed to be admitted to Soviet universities, Michael had managed to get a doctoral degree in physics. That was as far as he could go, though—every application to study astronomy had been turned down by the government.

In 1977, Michael had been able to go to Warsaw, Poland, to attend a mathematics conference. While Poland and the other Eastern European Soviet bloc countries might have been considered repressive by Western standards, by Soviet standards the intellectual atmosphere in Warsaw was relatively free. After meeting and talking to scientists from other European countries, Michael decided that he could no longer stay in the Soviet Union. He believed that his son Sergey would have a much better future in the United States.

In September 1978, the family applied to be allowed to leave the Soviet Union. The government's reaction was predictable: Michael was immediately fired from his job at GOSPLAN. The Brins had to scramble to find temporary work to make ends meet. They were also afraid that their son might be mistreated as a consequence of their decision. Instead of sending five-year-old Sergey to the government-run preschool, they kept him home.

May 1979 brought a stroke of luck: The government approved the Brins' application for an exit visa. This was an unusually swift response—indeed, many other Soviet Jews never had their visas approved and remained in a limbo for years, outcasts in their own society. (Not long afterward, in fact, the Soviet government stopped Jewish emigration entirely.)

## BECOMING AMERICAN

The Brins' journey to the United States took place in stages. The family first went to Vienna, Austria, and then spent a few months in Paris, France, where Michael took a temporary job to help the family pay for its journey. On October 25, 1979, the family arrived at Kennedy Airport in New York City. Some friends who had already emigrated picked them up and took them to their home in Long Island.

Michael was able to find a job teaching mathematics at the University of Maryland and the family settled into their new apartment—a bit cramped by American standards but considerably more spacious than what they had had in Moscow.

It was then that young Sergey, like Larry, encountered the rich learning environment of a Montessori school. There he and other preschoolers were offered a varied assortment of puzzles, building blocks, shapes, and other objects that allowed children to gain math and reading skills almost effortlessly.

At first, though, Sergey felt isolated from the other children. Although he knew a fair amount of English, his Russian accent made it hard for others to understand him. Soon, like generations of immigrant children before him, Sergey picked up American patterns of speech and culture.

## PROGRAMMING, MATH, AND SCIENCE

When he was nine, Sergey's parents gave him a Commodore 64 personal computer. Although not very powerful by modern standards, the machine's colorful graphics and sound capabilities were perfect for playing games.

These early PCs also came with BASIC, a simple computer programming language, and Sergey was soon writing his own computer adventure game.

In an interview for the American Academy of Achievement, Sergey recalls his wide-ranging exploration of the capabilities of the computer:

> In middle school, I had a very good friend who I'm still in touch with, he had a Macintosh, one of the early ones, and he and I would just sit and play around and program. We had little programs for artificial intelligence. We'd have a program that would talk back to you. We wrote a program to simulate gravity. I remember we wrote a program to do what's called "OCR" now, optical character recognition. It was just for fun, purely out of intellectual curiosity. I think that's probably the first time I really experienced that.

Sergey's talent for mathematics also proved to be remarkable. He began to listen in as his father discussed mathematics with colleagues from the university. One time they were discussing a difficult problem that had baffled their college students. Young Sergey could not restrain himself: He spoke up with a solution. At first the adults seemed not to have heard him. However, moments later one of them realized that Sergey had been right!

By age 15, Sergey probably knew more math than his high school teachers. He began taking classes at the University of Maryland while completing his high school requirements a year early.

While not very religious, the Brins did value their Jewish culture. Sergey went to a Hebrew school for three years. At age 11, Sergey went on a trip to Israel. However, he did not have a bar mitzvah, the ceremony in which a Jewish boy is acknowledged by the community to be on the threshold of adulthood. The gifts and other extravagances that usually accompanied the ceremony did not appeal to him.

Science in general had a strong appeal for Sergey. He enjoyed reading about famous scientists and how they made their discoveries. A particular role model was Richard Feynman (1918–88), the American physicist who helped work on the atomic bomb during World War II and who went on to develop quantum electrodynamics (QED), a key part of the quantum theory that explains the behavior of subatomic particles. But it was more than just Feynman's scientific achievements that appealed to young Sergey:

> It seemed like a very great life he led. Aside from making really big contributions in his own field, he was pretty broad-minded. I remember he had

an excerpt where he was explaining how he really wanted to be a Leonardo (Da Vinci), an artist and a scientist. I found that pretty inspiring. I think that leads to having a fulfilling life

Propelled by his interest and talent in math and science, Brin needed only three years to complete his undergraduate degree at the University of Maryland. Attracted to Stanford by its fine computer science program, Brin decided that it would be the perfect place to earn his doctoral degree in computer science.

Interestingly, though, Brin at first seemed more involved with sports such as skiing and inline skating. Strong and agile, Brin also found that he was quite good at gymnastics. One time when his father asked him if he had enrolled in any advanced classics, Brin replied only half-jokingly: "Yes, advanced swimming." Now socially confident and rather outgoing, Brin was invited to be a guide for prospective Stanford students. It was this that would lead to meeting and beginning to collaborate with Larry Page.

# Crawling the Web

As Brin and Page hiked around San Francisco together, they did not seem to get along very well. Page later recalled for John Battelle's article in *Wired* that "Sergey is pretty social; he likes meeting people." However Page thought that Brin "was pretty obnoxious. He had really strong opinions about things, and I guess I did, too." Nevertheless, Page and Brin seemed impressed with one another's quickness and intelligence and enjoyed their arguments/discussions. (Battelle describes them as "two swords sharpening one another.")

That fall Page returned to Stanford, having enrolled as a graduate student in computer science. "At first, it was pretty scary," he recalled in the spring/summer 2001 *Michigan Engineer*. "I kept complaining to my friends that I was going to get sent home on the bus. It didn't quite happen that way, however."

## BEGINNING A PARTNERSHIP

By his second semester, Page was settling in to campus life. Although he and Brin had different offices in Stanford's new William Gates Computer Science center, Page's room soon became an impromptu headquarters for him, Brin, and several other graduate students. Filled with computers, a sleeping mat, and even a piano, Room 360 at Gates became a 24-hour hub of furious work punctuated by equally intense (and sometimes silly) rambling discussions and arguments. Page's happiness in this new environment was marred only by the death of his father from pneumonia.

# WHAT IF WE COULD DOWNLOAD THE WHOLE WEB?

Computer science offered many exciting research topics in such areas as artificial intelligence (AI), pattern recognition, and image processing. But Page's adviser, Terry Winograd (1946–   ), though a pioneer in AI, suggested that his eager graduate student look at something else—the *World Wide Web*.

First developed in the early 1990s by Tim Berners-Lee (1955–   ), the World Wide Web had, by the end of its first decade, grown into a rapidly expanding universe of linked sites representing many thousands of businesses and other organizations and a growing number of individuals.

Berners-Lee had made the protocols, or rules, for formatting and linking Web pages freely available. No one needed permission to create Web sites— just some freely available software and a hosting service to store the data on its servers. Likewise, there were no rules about what pages a particular page could link to. This freedom allowed the Web to grow without restraint and

The newly built William Gates Computer Science building at Stanford University was the scene for Page and Brin's pioneering research on Web links. *(GlPhotoStockZ/Alamy)*

tried to find the best ways to meet their
ʼucational, or social.

ʼucture also made it hard to analyze and
nks, which were beginning to rival the
ʼs in the human brain.

a 2009 address to the graduating
ʼ ne had a fateful dream:

ʼ up, I was thinking: what if we could download the
ʼust keep the links and . . . I grabbed a pen and started writ-
ʼetimes it is important to wake up and stop dreaming. I spent the
ʼiddle of that night scribbling out the details and convincing myself it
would work.

What did Brin conclude from this experience? As he advised a new generation of Michigan students: "When a really great dream shows up, grab it!"

"So optimism is important," he went on. "You have to be a little silly about the goals you are going to set. There is a phrase I learned in college called, 'Having a healthy disregard for the impossible,'" Page said. "That is a really good phrase. You should try to do things that most people would not."

Page calculated that he should be able to download everything on the Web in about two weeks. Eagerly, he told Winograd about his project. Winograd was quite encouraging, even though he knew the Web was already much bigger than Page had realized.

When Page told Brin about his Web idea, Brin was also intrigued. Brin's own computer science specialty was *data mining,* or the identification of patterns and relationships within masses of data. Usually this data would be limited to a particular type. For example, Amazon.com has become famous for its ability to offer buyers suggestions for additional purchases. To do so, Amazon looks at, among other things, what other customers who have bought certain items go on to buy later. In turn, whatever someone chooses to purchase becomes part of the data used to figure out how to entice others to buy that product.

Page's idea, though, would be data mining on a far vaster scale—that of the entire Web. As recalled in John Battelle's *The Search,* Brin decided that Page's project would become his as well:

I talked to lots of research groups, and this was the most inte[...] both because it tackled the Web, which represents human kn[...] because I liked Larry and the other two people who were workin[...]

Page and Brin obtained initial funding from the Stanford Digi[...] Project (SDLP), in turn funded by the National Science Foundatio[...]

## THE INQUIRING MIND OF TIM BERNERS-LEE

Tim Berners-Lee (1955–   ) invented the linked system of data on the *Internet* that would become known as the World Wide Web. He later recalled that as a child he was fascinated by a how-to book called *Enquire Within Upon Everything*, which answered, in the form of an encyclopedia, questions on diverse topics such as etiquette, laundry tips, and first aid—for example, how to: cure a headache, get married, or bury a relative. Berners-Lee named his program that was the precursor to the Web ENQUIRE after this book, whose title suggested a magic doorway to the world. While he trained as a physicist, he maintained a keen interest in the organization and retrieval of knowledge.

After graduating from Oxford University and working at CERN, the European Organization for Nuclear Research, Berners-Lee struggled with organizing the dozens of incompatible computer systems and software that had been brought to the labs by thousands of scientists from around the world. With existing systems each requiring a specialized access procedure, researchers had little hope of finding out what their colleagues were doing or of learning about existing software tools that might solve their problems.

Berners-Lee's solution was to bypass traditional database systems and to consider text on all systems as "pages" that would each have a unique address, a Universal Document Identifier (later known as a Uniform Resource Locator, or *URL*). He and his assistants used existing ideas of hypertext to link words and phrases on one page to another page and adapted existing hypertext editing software for the NeXT computer to create the first World Wide Web pages, a server to provide access to the pages and a simple browser, a program that could be used to read pages and follow the links as the reader desired. Two standards would define al grant, the SDLP's goal was described as "to provide an infrastructure affords interoperability among heterogeneous, autonomous digital ry services." Translated into simpler language, this meant that since the s large amounts of text and other data had been stored in a variety of *bases*. Each database had its own format and rules for searching it. This nt it was very difficult for anyone except a trained specialist to find

how the system worked: *HTTP* (hypertext transfer protocol) would specify how pages were requested and provided to users, while *HTML* (hypertext markup language) would control the organization and formatting of the pages and elements such as links and graphics. But while existing hypertext systems were confined to browsing a single file or, at most, the contents of a single computer system, Berners-Lee's World Wide Web used the emerging Internet to provide nearly universal access.

Between 1990 and 1993, word of the Web spread throughout the academic community as Web software was written for more computer platforms. As demand grew for a body to standardize and shape the evolution of the Web, Berners-Lee founded the World Wide Web Consortium (W3C) in 1994. Together with his colleagues, he has struggled to maintain a coherent vision of the Web in the face of tremendous growth and commercialization, the involvement of huge corporations with conflicting agendas, and contentious issues of censorship and privacy. His general approach has been to develop tools that would empower the user to make the ultimate decision about the information he or she would see or divulge.

Berners-Lee also coined the term *semantic web* to refer to systems for embedding special information (metadata) within Web pages, enabling programs to access appropriate pages and work with them automatically.

Today, Berners-Lee's projects include working with a British government task force to make most government-collected data freely available to researchers and other users. In November 2009, Berners-Lee launched the World Wide Web Foundation in order to "Advance the Web to empower humanity by launching transformative programs that build local capacity to leverage the Web as a medium for positive change."

Berners-Lee was knighted by Queen Elizabeth II in 2004, with the rank of Knight Commander of the Most Excellent Order of the British Empire.

anything. What they were trying to find was a way to access all these data sources using the same user interface.

What Page and Brin realized is that thanks to Berners-Lee and his World Wide Web, there was already a potential way to share virtually any kind of data and make it accessible to everyone. What was needed was a way to provide an *index* to the Web, and a way for people to search for the information they wanted.

## THE FIRST SEARCH ENGINES

In 1996, there were only around 35 million Web users and about 300,000 Web sites, but these numbers were growing at a rapidly accelerating rate. As of 2011, the Web had more than 2 billion users and about 800 million distinct Web addresses were in existence. Indeed, the system of Web addressing has had to be expanded to accommodate the seemingly inexhaustible demand.

Like other Web users of the time, Page and Brin were familiar with the problem of finding information online. There was basically one approach in use, and it was increasingly failing. As the Web grew, it had become clear that it needed the equivalent of an index that would enable users to find sites that were likely to contain the information they were seeking. By the mid-1990s, there were a number of *search engines*—programs that could take a user's word or phrase and return a list of matching Web pages.

The basic operation of these early search engines was pretty straightforward if quite tedious. One part was the *Web crawler* (or, inevitably, "spider") that was essentially an automatic browser that tried to find every available Web page by patiently following link after link. As each page was encountered, it was read, and its keywords and phrases were added to a massive index, rather like the one at the end of a book. Finally there was the *user interface,* which gave the user a place to type the search words and a place to display the list of results. At the time, the most widely used Web search engine was called Altavista.

While these early search engines could retrieve useful results, they were always in danger of being overwhelmed. By the time a crawler finished its scouring of the Web, there would be thousands of new sites and tens of thousands of pages and links that would have been missed. Even using multiple crawlers and setting them to follow different but overlapping paths could not ensure that coverage would be up to date.

The other problem was at the user end. The more the Web grew, the more sites would be found for a given search *query.* The user needed some

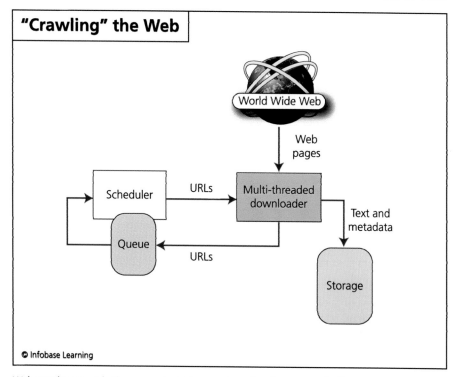

## "Crawling" the Web

World Wide Web

Web pages

Scheduler

URLs

Multi-threaded downloader

Text and metadata

Queue

URLs

Storage

© Infobase Learning

Web crawlers provide the raw material for search engines by systematically retrieving and storing the contents of Web pages.

way to determine which of perhaps thousands of "hits" represented pages on which the information was truly relevant and credible.

Suppose, for example, someone wanted information about a disease. The list of hits might be random or perhaps arranged according to how many times a *keyword* such as "flu" appeared on the page. Among the first sites listed might be one from the Mayo Clinic or the federal Centers for Disease Control—but there might also be a site from someone claiming that the flu epidemics were being caused by aliens seeking to cripple and conquer the Earth—or more likely, people promoting dubious pills or other treatments. Often, therefore, the results of Web searches were not nearly as useful as the searcher might have hoped.

## BACKRUB AND PAGERANK

In most cases, early Web search engines only used links to crawl from page to page and site to site across the Web. What Page and Brin realized is that the links actually contained valuable information. A link means that someone considers the site or page being linked to be useful. Sites to which many other sites link are more likely to be of high quality.

Page and Brin had picked the right time to begin to explore the Web systematically. The Web was now large enough to be very interesting but still small enough that all the links could be retrieved and stored for later use.

Page therefore created a new kind of Web crawler, which he dubbed BackRub. Instead of following links forward to other pages, it would follow them backward via *backlinks*. Page's new Web analyzer for the first time made it possible to look at a Web page and quickly determine what other pages linked to it.

This was the beginning of tackling a problem that was increasingly frustrating scientists. The days when a scientist could read or keep track of all the scientific papers that might be relevant to his or her specialty were long gone. Not only were there an ever-increasing number of scientific journals, but papers were starting to show up on the Web before being printed. There had to be a way to find within this flood of publications the papers whose links meant that they were considered important by recognized professionals.

A good start was to turn BackRub into a search engine. Instead of just listing matching pages in a more or less random order, BackRub listed them with the most linked-to pages first. Even that simple tweak gave results that were considerably more useful than those provided by Altavista and its competitors.

This was only the first step. Not all Web links are created equal. A link to a science page from a science museum, for example, is more important than a link from a third grade student who is doing a science project. But how can one tell which of the incoming links are more important? The answer is to go to the page from which the backlink is coming and see how many pages are linked to that page in turn.

In other words, this process involves recursion, an important topic in computer science. In simple terms, recursion is applying a procedure (or *algorithm*) to its own results, over and over again until some stopping point is reached. This was a key insight for turning the "backlink crawler" into what would become known as the *PageRank* algorithm.

As Page and Brin explained in their paper "The Anatomy of a Large-Scale Hypertextual Web Search Engine" in 1998:

PageRank relies on the uniquely democratic nature of the web by using its vast link structure as an indicator of an individual page's value. In essence,

Google interprets a link from page A to page B as a vote, by page A, for page B. But, Google looks at considerably more than the sheer volume of votes, or links a page receives; for example, it also analyzes the page that casts the vote. Votes cast by pages that are themselves "important" weigh more heavily and help to make other pages "important." Using these and other factors, Google provides its views on pages' relative importance.

But how could such a complex structure of links and backlinks be manipulated to give useful search results? It is here that Brin's particular talent for math came in handy. There is a whole branch of mathematics called graph theory. This kind of graph is not like the plots with X and Y coordinates that are familiar to high school students. Rather, this kind of graph

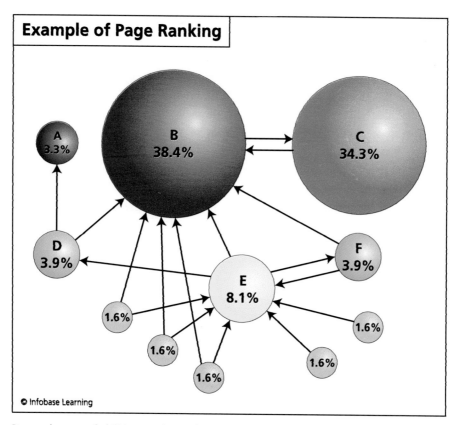

**Example of Page Ranking**

A
3.3%

B
38.4%

C
34.3%

D
3.9%

F
3.9%

E
8.1%

1.6%

1.6%

1.6%

1.6%

1.6%

1.6%

© Infobase Learning

Page rank uses probabilities to estimate the percentage of time users will click on a link to a given page. However, the links are also weighted according to an estimate of the page's relative value or importance. For this reason, here page C has a much higher page rank than page E, even though page E has more pages linking to it.

refers to a structure made of nodes (usually represented by circles) connected by links. This structure fits perfectly into the scheme of the Web, which consists of documents (pages) as nodes that are connected by links. However, the huge equation that sums up the nodes and links has hundreds of variables to manipulate. Brin had to find a procedure that would work yet also be feasible given the computing resources available.

In the decade following the invention of PageRank, the algorithm has been further refined and combined with many other procedures in Google's search engines.

## FROM BACKRUB TO GOOGLE

Stanford had a *Web server* of course. Page and Brin installed BackRub on it and began to tell other students and faculty at Stanford about their new search engine.

In early 1997, Page described BackRub on its home page:

Some Rough Statistics (from August 29th, 1996)
Total indexable HTML urls: 75.2306 Million
Total content downloaded: 207.022 gigabytes

. . .

BackRub is written in Java and Python and runs on several Sun Ultras and Intel Pentiums running Linux. The primary database is kept on an Sun Ultra II with 28GB of disk. Scott Hassan and Alan Steremberg have provided a great deal of very talented implementation help. Sergey Brin has also been very involved and deserves many thanks.
—Larry Page page@cs.stanford.edu

Word quickly spread that two graduate students had come up with a better way to find things on the Web.

By modern standards, BackRub was tiny. The total downloaded content of 207 gigabytes is now exceeded by some peoples' personal MP3 music collections. The 28 GB of disk space on the database server is less than the memory available in many of today's smartphones and tablets. Nevertheless, Page and Brin already had several machines and were developing ways to expand or *scale up* their system, which was based on the free, *open-source* Linux operating system, and used freely available programming languages.

Page and Brin decided that if their service were to be taken seriously by businesses and other institutions it should have a better name than the descriptive but "punny" BackRub. Page began to ask colleagues for suggestions, but he was not happy with any of them.

One day, though, his colleague Sean Anderson suggested "Googleplex." "Googol" had been invented many years ago as the name for a number consisting of $10^{100}$—that is, 10 followed by one hundred zeroes. Even that number was not large enough for the mathematical imagination, so along came googolplex, defined as 10 followed by a googol's worth of zeroes. This inconceivable number amounts to far more than the total number of particles in the known universe and writing it out would require more space than is available in the whole universe.

Brin liked the idea, but he suggested a simpler form: Google. (At first he did not realize that they were misspelling Googol). He found that no Web domain name called Google had been registered, so they could secure it for their site. (Ironically, if they had known how to spell googol and searched for it, they would have found that the name spelled that way had already been taken.)

Google was still just a program running on a Stanford server. As the Web grew, so did Google's index database. As more people used Google for more searches, the lines connecting Stanford to the Internet began to jam. Other researchers and administrators were becoming annoyed.

Page and Brin needed to find their own servers to run Google. Today, powerful desktop computers with several gigabytes of memory cost only a few hundred dollars, while less than $100 buys a hard drive that can store a terabyte (1 trillion bytes of data). In the late 1990s, though, considerably less powerful computers and more modest amounts of disk space were priced in the hundreds and thousands of dollars.

Meanwhile, back in Stanford, computers began to pile up in their office in the Gates building, and even in Page's dorm room. Brin's room became the office for what was beginning to resemble an actual business. They received a grant for $10,000 from some sympathetic Stanford professors, but it wasn't enough to feed the insatiable need for space for the Web index. They maxed out all their credit cards and asked their parents if they could use theirs as well. They also announced what they were doing to the campus community:

> Google the research project has become Google.com. We want to bring higher quality and greatly improved search to the world, and a company seems to be the best vehicle for accomplishing that goal. We've been hiring more staff and putting up more servers to scale the system (we've started

ordering our computers in 21 packs). We've also begun crawling more often, so our results not only remain fast, they also remain up to date. We are rapidly hiring talented people to bring the latest and greatest technology to the Web.

According to Vise and Malseed:

Brin and Page offered ten reasons to work for Google, including cool technology, stock options, free snacks and drinks, and the proposition that millions of people "will use and appreciate your software."

Meanwhile, though, Page and Brin would have to find enough business for their business to be successful.

# On Their Own

Page and Brin faced a choice. What had started out as an interesting research project seemed to have the potential to become a big business—perhaps the next big thing on the Internet at a time when companies such as Amazon and eBay were beginning to attract news stories—and investors.

As quoted by Douglas Edwards, Brin was optimistic about the future, but far from specific:

> "I had lunch with Sergey and another engineer and it was clear they had a search engine," said engineer Ed Karrels, who in 1999 was trying to decide if he should leave SGI for a job at Google, "but everybody and their brother had a search engine in those days. I asked, 'Where are you going with this? How will you make money?' And Sergey said, 'Well . . . , we'll figure something out.' I asked, 'Do you already have a plan figured out and you're collecting smart people to make it happen?' And he said, 'Yeah, that's pretty much it.'" Very reassuring.

One alternative would be to license their search technology to an existing company. They might receive an impressive amount of money, their Google technology would be out there benefiting millions of Web users, and their reputation as computer scientists would also be secure.

Page and Brin began to tour Silicon Valley, demonstrating Google to companies and explaining how their algorithm gave search results that were much more reliable and useful. The problem was that businesses could not figure out how having a better search engine would actually translate into their making more money. Web users were not about to pay to use a search engine when plenty of alternatives were available for free. Search might entice people to one's Web site, but once they were there, they would have to do something else that could provide a source of revenue—that is, could *monetize* the site.

*Yahoo,* for example, was trying to make money by selling advertising that would be shown to its users. Their main way of attracting users was to provide their own index of carefully selected and organized Web links— such a site is known as a *Web portal* because it is a kind of gate to destinations on the Internet. The two entrepreneurs who had founded Yahoo, Jerry Yang (1968–   ) and David Filo (1966–   ), focused mainly on creating a rich, attractive portal offering a vast variety of well-organized Web links together with news, e-mail, and other services. They already had a search engine, and it seemed good enough for their purposes. Rather dismissively, they thanked Page and Brin for their interesting demo and suggested that they simply create their own business. They did not think that Google would ever be a competitive threat to their established Web portal. After all, Google was just a search engine.

## A FATEFUL DECISION

Good software is not created all at once. It results from a continuous process of collecting feedback from users, finding and fixing bugs, and evaluating requests for new features. During the first part of 1998, Page and Brin refined Google's interface. For example, they added a bit of text from the linked page to each search result, enabling the user to glance through the list and find those items most likely to be relevant.

Vise and Malseed note that by July 1998 Google announced that its index now contained 24 million Web pages. They urged their growing body of users to "Have fun and keep googling." (Already, it seems google was turning into a verb.)

As the number of search requests passed 10,000 a day, a new problem arose. In addition to needing a constant supply of new computers and hard drives for storing the growing index, the requests had to pass through Stanford's Internet connections and be processed on the machine connected to the www.stanford.edu Web site. Finally, the day came when the whole Stanford computer network crashed under the load.

It was time for a crucial decision. If Google were to continue, it would have to have its own Internet domain and computing site off the Stanford campus. Running Google would have to become a full-time job. But Page and Brin had worked hard toward their degrees. Their innovations in Web analysis and search were certainly first-class computer science work. Should they (perhaps temporarily) shut down Google, write their dissertations, and then launch their business? As quoted by Vise and Malseed, one of their professors, Jeffrey Ullman, urged them not to abandon Google just when it was starting to become a presence on the Web. After all, he said, "You guys can always come back and finish your Ph.Ds if you don't succeed."

## FUEL FOR LAUNCH

Without the facilities and modest grants from the university, where would Google get the money to set up shop? Existing Web companies had not been willing to buy or license their software. Somehow they had to find an investor or *venture capitalist* who would be willing to give them money in exchange for a stake in their company.

Personal contacts and luck often determine whether a *start-up* company such as Google get the money they need. In this case, David Cheriton, one of Page's professors, knew Andy von Bechtolsheim, a Stanford graduate and cofounder of Sun Microsystems, a multibillion dollar developer of high performance computer work stations and software. Cheriton suggested that Page and Brin get in touch with Bechtolsheim.

Bechtolsheim quickly responded to Brin's e-mail. Yes, he was interested in Google and its search engine. Could they meet the next morning? They agreed to meet at Professor Cheriton's house.

Page and Brin arrived and waited on Cheriton's porch. As Page recalled to Battelle:

> David [Cheriton] had a laptop on his porch in Palo Alto, with an Ethernet connection. We did a demo, and Andy asked a lot of questions. [Then] he said: "Well, I don't want to waste time. I'm sure it'll help you guys if I just write a check."

There had been none of the usual venture capitalist questions, such as, "What is your business plan?," or "What do you estimate is the size of your market?" Normally, before a venture capitalist makes an offer of financing in return for a share in the company, there has to be an estimate of the valuation, or likely worth of the company. Page and Brin, however, had not even thought about that little matter.

As Bechtolsheim walked back to his car to get his checkbook, Page and Brin frantically tried to come up with a number for the valuation. When Bechtolsheim returned, they told him their number, and, as Brin recalls, the investor replied, "Oh, I don't think that's enough, I think it should be twice that much." Bechtolsheim began to write out a check for $100,000, asking who it should be made out to. Page and Brin had also not thought about what they would call their business. At Bechtolsheim's suggestion, they decided on Google, Inc.

Page carefully put the check in his dorm room desk drawer. They could not cash it, because Google, Inc., did not even exist yet. They had to file papers to incorporate and obtain company bank accounts. On September 7, 1998, Google, Inc., finally came into existence. Page would be the chief executive officer (CEO) and Brin the president. They then hired their first employee, fellow student Craig Silverstein.

Next they needed an office. It turned out that Susan Wojcicki, a friend of a friend, had bought a house in Menlo Park near the Stanford campus. She

The original garage office of Google, rented from Susan Wojcicki, who later became an important Google executive  (AP Images)

was worried about making the mortgage payments and agreed to rent the garage to Brin and Page. They moved in, along with Silverstein.

## BIG IDEAS, SMALL SPACES

The garage was soon packed with stacks of computers, tables, and chairs. Their desks were wooden doors laid across sawhorses. Keeping the garage door open provided needed ventilation so the servers would not overheat.

The combination of hard work and zany fun characteristic of graduate students did not go away, despite their new business responsibilities. When technology writer Steven Levy had his first interview with Page and Brin in 1998, it happened to be on Halloween:

> Larry was dressed as a Viking, with a long-haired furred vest and a hat with long antlers protruding. Sergey was in a cow suit. On his chest was a rubber slab from which protruded huge, wart-specked teats. They greeted me cheerfully and we all retreated to a conference room where the Viking and the cow explained the miraculous powers of Google's PageRank technology.

As the Web crawlers ground away, about 100 pages a second were fetched from the Web and indexed. As word of mouth spread beyond Stanford, the number of Google users also grew rapidly. Google was becoming news. In December 1998, *PC Magazine* named Google one of its top 100 Web sites and search engines. According to Steven Levy in a 1999 article for *Newsweek,* "Google, the Net's hottest search engine, draws on feedback from the Net itself to deliver more relevant search results to customer queries." As Google grew, it soon outgrew the garage, and they found office space in nearby Palo Alto.

Douglas Edwards quotes Urs Hölzle, Google's head of engineering, as he explains what was happening:

> Speed or scale. Pick one. When we crawled more web pages, the index got bigger and the pageranker had more data to draw upon, so we could produce more-relevant results. That attracted more users and more searches, so our audience grew. A bigger index, however, required more machines doing more processing, and more processing took more time. Adding users puts more demand on the network, which, as anyone sharing an Internet connection knows, slows things down.

But as Edwards went on to note, "Larry and Sergey chose both. Google's quest would be to get faster even as it expanded in both directions."

## SCROUNGING SERVERS AND PACKING CAGES

By necessity, the two undergraduates became scroungers and improvisers. Larry recalled that they would watch the university's loading dock for boxes from computer companies. If such a box lay around for awhile and no one picked it up, "We would just borrow a few machines," Page would tell Vise and Malseed, "figuring that if they didn't pick it up right away, they didn't need it so badly."

According to Douglas Edwards in *I'm Feeling Lucky,* the thrifty habits Page and Brin were forced to adopt while still at Stanford would become an integral part of the Google culture:

> "Build machines so cheap that we don't care if they fail. And if they fail, just ignore them until we get around to fixing them." That was Google's strategy, according to hardware designer Will Whitted, who joined the company in 2001. "That concept of using commodity parts and of being extremely fault tolerant, of writing the software in a way that the hardware didn't have to be very good, was just brilliant." But only if you could get the parts to fix the broken computers and keep adding new machines. Or if you could improve the machines' efficiency so you didn't need so many of them.

In the next few years, Google would have regular events called Cable-Fests where employees (even nontechnical marketing people) would be expected to lend a hand assembling and cabling together new servers. The servers were kept in huge warehouselike "collocation facilities" or "server farms." Douglas Edwards described what one of these places looked like:

> Imagine an enormous, extremely well-kept zoo, with chain-link walls draped from floor to ceiling creating rows of large fenced cages vanishing somewhere in the far, dark reaches of the Matrix. Inside each cage is a mammoth case (or several mammoth cases) constructed of stylish black metal and glass, crouched on a raised white-tile floor into which cables dive and resurface like dolphins. Glowing green and red lights flicker as disks whir, whistle, and stop, but no human voices are ever heard as frigid air pours out of exposed ceiling vents and splashes against shiny surfaces and around hard edges.

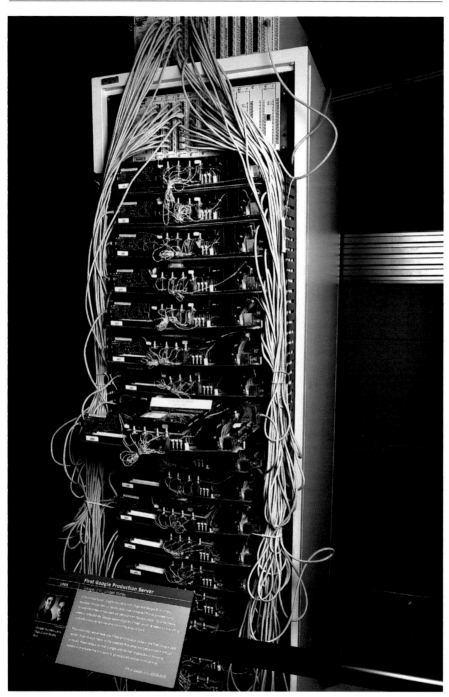

Google's first production server sits on display at the Computer History Museum in Mountain View, California. *(Tony Avelar/Bloomberg, via Getty Images)*

Page and Brin had an insight into the economics of such facilities, and it would end up saving them hundreds of thousands of dollars. Space was rented by the square foot, and the rent included the cost of power for the machines and a sufficient amount of air conditioning to keep them from overheating. Typically, a company (such as the search engine Inktomi) might fit 50 servers into a standard-sized cage. Google, however, stripped away the machine's cases, reconfigured the circuit boards, fans, and vents, and crammed 1,500 servers into the same space! Even though they had 30 times as many machines as a typical user, they did not have to pay any extra for power or other facilities.

One day the team working on the servers included Jim Reese, a former neurosurgeon who had hired on at Google as a system administrator, and Larry Schwimmer, an engineer who worked on Google's e-mail service and security system. One engineer pointed out that if one row of server cabinets could be shifted just three inches, another rack (containing 80 machines) could be squeezed in. It would mean temporarily removing the side wall from the cage, but after that was done, they had moved everything, slid the new rack in, and wired all the machines up. Everything was fine—until a ceiling beam, which had not been properly refastened, crashed down on Reese. As quoted by Douglas Edwards:

> "Uh . . . ," said Jim, shakily pointing upward toward a batch of severed cables that had lain in the beam's path, "we're going to need more fiber." "You're the only neurosurgeon around," replied Schwim, assessing the situation with both concern and an engineer's practicality. "Do you think you can fix yourself?"

Assembling and managing an impromptu network of Web servers, database programs, and storage systems helped Page and Brin understand how to squeeze every last byte of space and increment of speed out of software and hardware. This ability to obtain efficiency while responding to the needs of growth would prove useful to them in coming years when Google bought computers not by the dozens but by the thousands.

## FINDING SUPPORT AND REACHING OUT

Google's growing fame finally began to attract serious investors. Two big venture capital firms, Kleiner Perkins and Sequoia Capital, each agreed to invest $12.5 million in Google. In talking to the press about this multimillion-dollar vote of confidence in Google, Page said that Google's plan was "to continue to provide the best search experience on the Web." Brin then chimed in: "A perfect search engine will process and understand all the information in the world. That is where Google is headed." Douglas Edwards goes on to describe Page and Brin's enthusiastic plans for Google:

> They would speed medical breakthroughs, accelerate the exploration of space, break down language barriers. Instead of putting a Band-Aid on global ignorance and confusion, they would clear the clogged arteries of the world's data systems and move information effortlessly to the point at which it was needed at exactly the time it was required.

This was certainly an ambitious goal. Meanwhile, if it was going to justify the investors' faith, Google would have to become a household name—at least for the millions of households who were getting connected to the Web, not to mention schools, libraries, and businesses of all sizes.

One person who would play an important role in making Google visible was Susan Wojcicki. It was her garage that had provided Google's first corporate home. Having earned her MBA in 1998 and with a strong interest in marketing, she was in the right place to go from being Google's landlady to becoming one of its first key employees.

Companies such as Microsoft and Yahoo used traditional advertising to keep their name in front of consumers. Yahoo, for example, bought millions of dollars worth of TV and radio ads, most with the tagline "Do you Yahoo?"

Wojcicki and the other Google marketers took a different approach. They realized early on what is commonplace knowledge today: The Web is a social medium. The best way to get more users is to motivate your existing users to spread the word about your service. Every time someone told a friend "Hey, look what I found on Google about this," chances were good that next time that friend needed some information he or she would try Google.

## FOOD FOR THOUGHT

By late 1999, Google had grown to 40 employees and needed more space. They moved to new quarters in Mountain View. While Page and Brin had been scrupulous about not wasting money on expensive equipment or advertising, they believed that investing in making employees' lives better and easier was not only the right thing to do, it would make them happier and, in the long run, more productive.

As a workplace, Google is famous for its combination of intense work and frequent opportunities to relax or play. Page *(left)* and Brin are relaxing here on beanbags at Google headquarters in Mountain View, California, in 2000. *(AP Images)*

The classic example was the company cafeteria. Where most companies might be satisfied with a glorified version of a school lunchroom, Page and Brin interviewed 25 gourmet chefs before choosing Charlie Ayers. Under his supervision, gourmet meals were available not only for lunch but also for breakfast and dinner—suiting the long hours for which the best programmers and software engineers were notorious. (In 2006, Ayers left Google to open his own restaurant in Palo Alto.)

Google's gourmet food would become only the first of a series of employee benefits that would make Google consistently rank as one of the best companies in America for which to work.

## GOOGLING YAHOO

As 2000 dawned, Google seemed to be on the brink of becoming the Web's next big thing. Just a couple of years earlier, when two Stanford graduate students named Brin and Page had shown their search engine around Silicon Valley, Yahoo's Jerry Yang and David Filo had said, essentially, "Thanks, but no thanks."

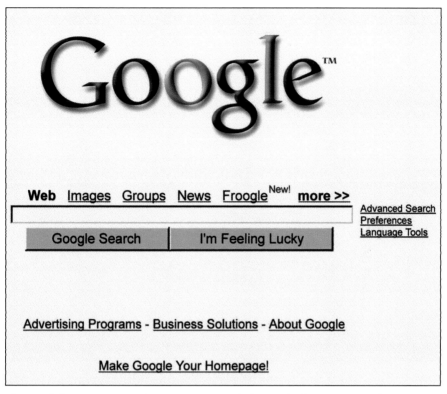

The Google home page is just about the most straightforward landing place one will ever find on the Web—though it includes a whimsical touch now and then. *(HO/AFP/Getty Images)*

Yahoo was primarily a portal, offering a carefully selected assortment of Web links that could be browsed by subject. Increasingly, though, users wanted the freedom and responsiveness of a search engine that could take them directly where they wanted to go. Yahoo did provide Web search, but it was through an engine they had licensed from a rather obscure company. It was far from state of the art.

In May 2000, after sometimes contentious negotiation, Google won the contract to handle Yahoo's search traffic. Google's engineers went into high gear—they would have only a month to ramp up Google's capacity so it could handle millions of search requests from users of the world's largest Web portal. It was no longer a matter of a single server farm, but data centers around the world, connected to a system that would do load balancing—shifting resources from moment to moment even as the peak traffic followed the Sun from Europe to North America to Asia.

Google is always trying to bring the most relevant and useful search results to the top of the list. Here a search for the FIFA soccer World Cup in 2010 brings scores and upcoming games. *(linx Photography Brands/Alamy)*

Typically, Page and Brin decided that Google would not only meet the challenge of serving Yahoo's huge customer base, they would also rev up the indexer in order to become the first search engine to index 1 billion Web addresses.

This meant they would have to change how the indexer worked. Originally, the crawler would do a complete run, compile, and index and then be started over to catch up with the new Web sites that were constantly appearing. The new crawler would be *incremental,* running all the time, constantly integrating the latest pages into the overall index. Meanwhile, there had to be enough machines both to do the indexing and to serve search results to users.

Finally, as the deadline approached, Douglas Edwards writes that

The machines were built, the data centers filled. The crawler had worked. The indexer had worked. The pageranker had worked. Google had identified a billion URLs and now could search them. We had the superior technology. The Yahoo deal proved we had the business smarts to go with it. It was time to take our light from under its bushel and show it to the world.

Despite Google's new stature as Yahoo's search engine and the world's biggest search provider, industry analysts seemed less than excited. CNET said that Google would not benefit much from this expansion because "the search market in general, meanwhile, remains a low-margin, commodity business." What most observers missed was that Google was going to shift its business model from selling search services to selling advertising in connection with search results.

## ADDING AOL

In early 2002, Google signed an agreement to provide the Internet service provider *Earthlink* with Google search facilities. But the big target was *America Online* (AOL). AOL predated the Web, starting back in the days of dial-up access. Its big advantage had been providing complete, relatively easy to use software that enabled any PC user with a modem to go online. AOL pioneered in services such as online chat and games and eventually reached a peak of 30 million users.

AOL was late in realizing the importance of the Internet and Web, however, and its user base began to decline as fast broadband cable and DSL connections began to become common by the 2000s. In 2002, AOL had been getting its Web search services from a company called Overture (originally called GoTo).

In their meetings with Google, AOL representatives seemed confident in their bargaining position—they were still the biggest player on the Internet. Google's employees, by now often calling themselves Googlers, on the other hand, were not impressed with AOL. Like most tech-savvy people, they looked down on AOL as a "walled garden"—a closed-off place designed to protect clueless "newbies" (new users) from the wild world of the Web even while steering them to certain services.

As the meetings began, AOL brought an army of negotiators, product managers, and lawyers—all dressed impeccably in suits. The casually dressed Googlers, on the other hand, were confident that their search and advertising technology was far ahead of the competition. They demonstrated how their search engine connected users to ads that were far more relevant than those served up by Overture.

Overture had guaranteed AOL a minimum of $10 million in revenue for ads *targeted* to the contents of its pages. If Google were to be given the contract, AOL wanted even more. Page and Brin were confident that Google's search engine could deliver all that was demanded—and more. However as Vise and Malseed recount, Eric Schmidt had misgivings:

> I was terrified . . . Larry and Sergey and I argued hard. I understood that if you ran out of cash, you were done. They were more willing to take risk than me. They turned out to be right.

In the midst of the negotiations, Overture sued Google, claiming that the system of bidding for ads used in their AdWords program was their *intellectual property*. This caused AOL to demand that Google guarantee that if they lost the suit and looked like they were heading for bankruptcy, they would turn over all their intellectual property (for everything, not just ad programs) to AOL.

Page, Brin, and Schmidt absolutely refused. They would not risk everything even for a potentially very profitable deal with AOL. AOL decided that they had gone too far in their demands. The two companies then settled down to agree on how much of a guarantee of revenue Google would give and how they would share the revenue (this information was not publicly released).

On May 1, 2002, Google search results began to appear on the screens of AOL users. As a result of all of its deals with Internet portals, Google now had more than 50 percent of the overall search market. The *Wall Street Journal* noted, "The America Online pact now establishes Google as a major competitor in the paid-listings market, which Overture had dominated."

It turned out Google would have no trouble meeting AOL's expectations. One reason was that Google was always trying to improve the quality of their search results and ads. As an example of how much a little thing can mean in a user interface, an engineer named John Bauer thought it might be a good idea for the ad to boldface the keyword the user had used in the search. This showed the user that the ad was indeed relevant—and four times as many users clicked on such ads!

The signing of Yahoo and AOL to multimillion-dollar deals was an impressive achievement, but Google's development of techniques for leveraging search to make advertising more effective—and profitable—had just begun.

products should be associated with. They would bid on those words in a complex auction process that takes into account both bids by other advertisers and a quality score based on the relevance and previous effectiveness of the ads. The advertisers could pay either a fee per thousand impressions (times the ad is shown) or *pay per click* (or *clickthrough*)—a better indication of actual effectiveness.

Google then arranges (through an algorithm) for placement of the ads when users search with those words. The ads show up as sponsored links either above or to the right of the main search results. In 2003, Google would expand AdWords to include placement of ads on a network of *affiliates* or participating sites.

Like many of Google's algorithms, the actual workings of AdWords are proprietary, or kept secret by the company. As a result a wide variety of experts claim to have figured out how to help advertisers gain a better placement for their ads, but the value of such services has been questioned.

Page and Brin did not originate the basic idea of *pay-per-click* ad auctions. Back in 1998, the idea had been presented by a company called *Goto.com,* later called Overture. In 2004, a patent dispute was settled by Google paying Yahoo (which had bought Overture) about 1 percent of its stock. Another important Google advertising program, developed about the same time, is *AdSense.* In this program, Web site owners decide which pages on their sites can be accompanied by ads. Google automatically serves the ads based on the content of the page, paying the site owners depending on how many clicks or impressions the ad receives. The importance of this program can be seen in the fact that in 2011 it accounted for 28 percent of Google's total revenue.

Measuring the effectiveness of ads had always been more an art than a science. But online, user response can actually be measured in physical terms: What links were clicked on? (The most useful measurement is actually the *clickthrough rate*—the percentage of users who are shown an ad who actually click on it to go through to the advertiser's site.) By 2005, Google had developed a tool called Google Analytics that enabled advertisers to determine how people were getting to their stores (from which advertising or referring pages), as well as the rate of success as measured by accesses to a page or actual sales.

The ability to control how much one paid for ads and to measure users' interest proved to be quite attractive. Despite the tough economic climate, Google's ad revenue began to grow. Google had apparently solved the problem of how to make a free search engine that made money.

# Getting Big

Searching Google cost users absolutely nothing. Licensing deals like the one with Yahoo did offer a way to make money from the search engine, but it was limited. The big question that had faced the Web portals and search engine companies since the late 1990s was how to sell advertising. After all, generations of media companies from newspapers to radio to television had earned much of their money by selling advertising space or commercials.

Google was essentially created by technologists, not marketers. Page and Brin knew little about the advertising business. In *I'm Feeling Lucky,* Douglas Edwards, who came to Google from a business rather than a technical background, recalled the sharp difference in thinking between marketers and engineers:

> I was equally sanguine about my first glimpse of the way the two departments approached problems. We in marketing wrote proposals, made suggestions, and looked for broad formal approval before moving ahead one step at a time. Our engineers made quick data-based decisions and implemented them. If data supported a particular option, they rationalized, it was the right choice to make. Data didn't lie. If the numbers said changing A to B would improve product X, why not do it now? This mindset drove much of the urgency at Google. Engineers knew how to make things better, and every hour, every minute, every second we delayed improvements,

Playfully posing in Mountain View in 2002, Page (*left*) and Brin are wearing identical suits . . . and sneakers. (*Michael Grecco/Getty Images*)

users had to endure sub-optimal interactions with our site. That was unacceptable.

The problem of marketing Google and making the advertising it placed more effective would pit advertising professionals against those pragmatic engineers. As with all established professions, advertising experts had principles that they believed needed to be followed, but were rules derived from print or radio or television still relevant on the Web? The engineers in turn had their data, but were they measuring the things that really mattered?

## A NEW WAY TO ADVERTISE

Finding a way to fit advertising to the new medium of the Internet and t Web was turning out to be surprisingly difficult. The simplest approach w to slap a changing series of *banner ads* across the top of each page on a We site. Usually the ads were unrelated to what the users were trying to find an were perceived as intrusive, distracting, or annoying.

Another approach used by early search engines was to let companies pay to have their companies listed first in the search results. If someone searches, for example, for laptop, and Dell Computer is willing to pay for results associated with that keyword, then perhaps Dell would be the first thing listed in the search results.

Page and Brin hated that idea with a passion. They believed that the value of a search engine depended not only on its technical excellence but on the trust that users could have in its objectivity. It was something like journalism: If a company could pay to have its products mentioned favorably in news stories, how could readers trust that the news was being presented fairly and accurately?

The Google philosophy insisted that any advertising shown in connection with a search should first be a benefit to the user (such as by showing relevant products) and only then benefit the advertiser and, through fees, add to Google's revenue.

## ADWORDS AND ADSENSE

During 2000, the stock market had a sharp downturn, fueled to a considerable extent by the bursting of the dot-com bubble of over-hyped Web-based companies. With companies in general making less money, they had less money available for advertising.

At a time when simply putting one's business online was no longer viewed as the road to instant success, advertisers became more skeptical about the value of online ads. An old adage in advertising (attributed to several different people) held that "I know that half my advertising budget is wasted . . . but I don't know which half." What was known was that to the extent that advertising could be targeted to the more likely buyers, it would be more effective.

Google developed its AdWords service as an attempt to make ads more effective by connecting them to what people were searching for online. The idea behind AdWords is that advertisers would decide what keywords their

## GAMING GOOGLE

As the Web grew and many sites that were similar began to go online, it became increasingly difficult to be sure that one's site would rank high and stand out in Web searches. In particular, how does one get to the top of a Google search result list?

Some things are fairly obvious. By putting appropriate keywords in strings called metatags, site developers can ensure Web crawlers will be more likely to properly categorize the site. Also, as Google explained, if one can get other high quality sites to link to one's new site, that is likely to make Google consider the site to be more relevant to searchers and thus rank it higher. (If one pays to have a Web site designed for one's business or organization, such measures should be included in the service.)

For people who need to go further, there is an industry called *Search Engine Optimization* (SEO). An SEO specialist can change the HTML coding and even the design of the site to make it easier for Google's crawler to process properly and more likely to be ranked higher.

All these techniques are considered perfectly okay by Google, but there is a whole range of other techniques that attempt to manipulate Google's algorithms to give a site an inappropriate ranking in search results. A simple example is keyword spamming, which, as the name suggests, involves stuffing a site with keywords designed to make it show up in unrelated searches. Thus, for example, someone searching for health information might find pornography instead. More sophisticated techniques include creating a vast array of bogus sites just so they can link to the site being optimized—link spamming or *google bombing.*

Google has tried to educate Web developers about what optimization techniques are considered appropriate, while devising sophisticated algorithms for detecting attempts to game the system and rejecting such sites.

In recent years, both legitimate optimization and Google gaming have become more difficult because Google now also uses information about each Web searcher's past searches and behavior to create personalized results.

## SEARCH FOR A CEO

As part of obtaining $25 million from the venture capitalists, Page and Brin had promised that they would hire a CEO with the necessary experience to run what was becoming a major business with international reach. (In addition to their deal with Yahoo, Google had recently brought out versions of its search engine in 10 major languages.)

John Doerr, one of Google's major backers, had convinced 46-year-old Eric Schmidt (1955–   ) to come in for an interview. Schmidt had been trained as an engineer and had served on the board of directors at Apple Computer, a company whose innovations in hardware and operating systems have often been compared to Google's achievements on the Web. Schmidt had also played a major role at Novell, the company that had dominated the networking of PCs before the growth of Internet-based networking. However, Schmidt was now in his late 40s, making him almost a senior figure in the youth-oriented high tech industry. At first, Schmidt was rather reluctant to get involved with a company being run by people half his age.

Eric Schmidt giving the keynote speech at the 2010 IFA technology trade fair in Berlin, Germany, in September 2010. Schmidt was CEO of Google from 2001 until April 2011, overseeing one of history's greatest corporate expansions. *(Sean Gallup/Getty Images)*

As Vise and Malseed quote him, Schmidt was rather taken aback by his first meeting with the Google founders:

> [Page and Brin] criticized every single technical point I made, and everything I was doing in my business. They argued that this was the stupidest thing they'd ever heard of. I was just floored. It was really arrogant.

While Schmidt was startled by Page and Brin's confrontational, rapid-fire style, he saw that they were bright, passionate, and direct. In turn, Page and Brin recognized that Schmidt had a scientific as well as a business background, in addition to extensive experience in the computer industry. When Page and Brin offered Schmidt the position of chairman of the board in March 2001, he accepted it as an exciting challenge. In August, Schmidt was named CEO.

Vise and Malseed quote Schmidt as recalling two things that Google needed from him:

> Not only was I CEO and chairman, but I was also an investor of real money. The company literally needed the cash. And they wanted to see a real commitment.

They then noted how much Google needed Schmidt's combination of industry knowledge and management skill:

> Schmidt arrived at Google to find a technology firm that nearly three years after its founding was being run by technologists who put enormous time into people and products and users, but spent as little money and time as possible on the details of internal management.

Although there would often be heated arguments between Schmidt and the Google founders, they were carried on in an atmosphere of mutual respect. One of Schmidt's first tasks was to sharpen the company's focus and set an overall agenda. In July 2002, Schmidt, according to Douglas Edwards, laid out the Google Great Company Five.

> . . . the areas we needed to get right in order to become a great company: global sales, strong brand and ethics, great financials, a good hiring process, and innovation.

By then, though, Google had faced a challenge none of them could have foreseen.

## THE DAY THE WEB GREW UP

Google employees coming to work on September 11, 2001, soon learned that this was not going to be an ordinary day. They watched the burning, collapsing World Trade Center in New York City and the smoking hole in the Pentagon in Washington, D.C. Checking online, they saw that the news Web sites such as those of CNN and the *New York Times* were becoming inaccessible as millions of Web users searched for the latest news of the tragedy.

Google put its experience in running large-scale Web services to work. They realized that Google, with its huge index of stored Web information, had become something like the backup drive for the Internet. They put links on google.com that let users access stored copies of news stories and other information. They also linked people searching for news about the fate of loved ones to the Red Cross and other sites.

While Google's actions were motivated mainly by a desire to be of assistance to fellow citizens, they would turn out to have an unexpected benefit for the company. As author Richard Wiggins wrote in his article for *First Monday* in October 2001, "By meeting user demand for trusted information related to September 11, Google has trained millions of people to expect Google.com to deliver breaking news." Although the Google home page would soon return to its sparse layout, about a year later Google was offering Google news, which users can customize as part of their browser home pages. Douglas Edwards recalled how he introduced the new service to Google users:

> I had written into the FAQ explaining Google news: "Google news is highly unusual in that it offers a news service compiled solely by computer algorithms without human intervention. Google employs no editors, managing editors, executive editors, or other ink-stained wretches."

## "DON'T BE EVIL"

By mid-2001, Google had grown to more than 200 employees. Page and Brin were concerned that size and momentum could lead to uncontrolled growth—perhaps Google would become just another giant tech company, with the bland regimentation that many associated with IBM or Microsoft.

Page and Brin tried to stay in touch with a core group of their most creative employees. One day, they were talking about what should be the guiding principles that would keep Google true to its founding vision. They started listing some key ideas and arguing about then. As John Battelle recounts in *The Search,* one employee, engineer Paul Buchheit, then broke in, saying, "All of these things can be covered by just saying don't be evil."

Douglas Edwards recounts an example of what Page considered to be an "evil" form of business:

"Frequent flier programs are evil," he said. "They are?" I didn't recall my Mileage Plus number ending in 666. "They incentivize people to take flights that are not the most direct or the cheapest, just so they can earn points. Their employers end up paying more, and people lose time traveling." Loyalty programs promoted loyalty above efficiency, and that was just wrong, wrong, wrong.

Edwards continues his account of his conversation with Page:

We spent the first fifteen minutes talking about what Google was not and what we would never do. Larry wanted Google to be "a force for good," which meant we would never conduct marketing stunts like sweepstakes, coupons, and contests, which only worked because people were stupid. Preying on people's stupidity, Larry declared, was evil.

If that sort of thing was "evil" what was the good that Google should be doing? If we did have a category, it would be personal information— handling information that is important to you. The places you've seen. Communications. We'll add personalization features to make Google more useful. People need to trust us with their personal information, because we have a huge amount of data now and will have much more soon.

"Don't be evil" soon began appearing on whiteboards and signs all around the Google offices. To this day, Page and Brin believe it captures the essence of how Google should operate. Of course, this would not end the questions that would arise as Google's influence over the Web and how people used it became more and more dominant.

For their part, Page and Brin seem to sincerely believe in their instinct for right and wrong. Usually, they find themselves in agreement about an issue. As Page noted to Ken Auletta in *Googled:* "If we both feel the same way, we're probably right. If we don't agree, it's probably a toss up." Half-seriously, he then added: "If we both agree and nobody else agrees with us, we assume we're right."

# Here, There, and Everywhere

The desire to find new ways to help people find needed information, as well as the desire to make more money, would lead to the expansion of Google's search technology into many new areas. In turn, this would begin to bring new challenges and questions about privacy and the ownership of information.

## LOCAL SEARCH AND GOOGLE MAPS

One of the earliest expansions of Google beyond general-purpose Web search was local search—providing information relevant to where the user lives or is traveling.

Starting in 2004, Google offered a feature called Google Local. The user typed in his or her location (today this is usually obtained automatically using *GPS* or nearby *wi-fi* hot spots). Next, the user typed in something to find locally, such as a restaurant or a hairdresser. The result is not just a series of links, but a map showing where each place is located.

Originally, the maps provided were rather rudimentary, but then along came Google Maps. In a pattern often to be repeated, this product did not originate inside Google but belonged to a company that Google acquired in 2004.

Maps represent a logical extension of search, by providing a different kind of information that could be used to explore, learn about an area, or

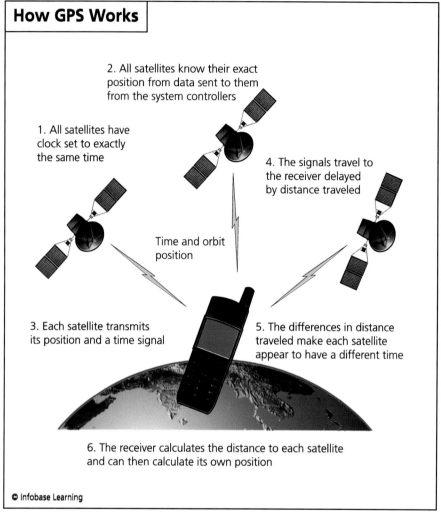

**How GPS Works**

1. All satellites have clock set to exactly the same time

2. All satellites know their exact position from data sent to them from the system controllers

3. Each satellite transmits its position and a time signal

4. The signals travel to the receiver delayed by distance traveled

5. The differences in distance traveled make each satellite appear to have a different time

Time and orbit position

6. The receiver calculates the distance to each satellite and can then calculate its own position

© Infobase Learning

Global positioning system (GPS) uses several satellites to pinpoint the location of a user. Google exploits this feature to provide mobile users with maps and other information relevant to their surroundings.

navigate (through providing driving directions, traffic information, and, eventually, routes for public transit or even walking). By integrating local search with Google Maps, the service provides a quick and easy way for both residents and travelers to find all the things they are searching for. Further, as a sort of interactive Yellow Pages, Google Maps and local search helped open a whole new market for Google's advertising services—small and local businesses for which Web-wide advertising was inappropriate or too expensive.

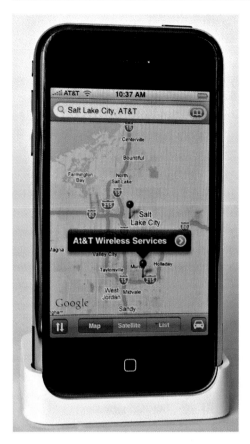

Google Maps on mobile devices have become an essential navigation tool for millions of travelers  *(George Frey/ Bloomberg via Getty Images)*

Google also provided users with a way to post reviews of businesses, an idea pioneered by Yelp, Inc. This creates a sort of virtuous circle, in which the site lets users create content (reviews) that in turn makes the site more useful to others, which in turn leads to more growth in the number of users.

By 2010, Google Maps had added many more features, thanks in part to a programming interface that makes it easy to create displays of one's own data from several sources, resulting in what are called *mashups*. Interesting displays can be created using only basic programming skill—for example, showing Twitter users and their posts or showing the location of apartment rentals from Craigslist.

## GOOGLE EARTH

It could have been a scene from an old science fiction movie set in the world of the 21st century. A woman holds a glowing slatelike object in her hand. It shows a blue globe of the Earth brilliant against a starry back-ground. With a few finger flicks she selects the West Coast of North Amer-ica, then the San Francisco Bay Area. As she touches the globe and pinches her fingers apart, the display expands at a dizzying rate. Now she hovers over Golden Gate Park and then follows her street. A few more flicks and the display switches to Street View, and there is her house in full, detailed color. She pans the image around and notices her neighbor is putting out the trash.

But this is not science fiction. It is Google Earth, a product first intro-duced in 2005 and steadily refined since. With detailed imagery for many cities around the world, as well as natural wonders, Google Earth provides a way to explore the world at one's own pace at any desired level of detail—or to become more familiar with a new neighborhood. For people seeking to explore farther afield, there are also detailed views of the Moon and Mars.

Google has added Street View to its maps of many urban areas—here, a laptop on a street in Essen, Germany, shows that very street. *(Julian Stratenschulte/EPA/Landov)*

Google Earth combines maps, actual scenery, and photos that have been geotagged with their coordinates, showing exactly where they were taken—in this case, the Swiss canton of Aargau. *(AP Images)*

For its earthbound imagery, Google sends out fleets of cars, each equipped with an array of nine special cameras, GPS units for precise location measurements, and laser range finders. The images are updated periodically, and it has become a popular pastime to try to guess when a given image may have been taken.

However, as with other products that have provided access to new worlds of information, Google Earth has also raised privacy concerns, particularly with regard to Street View, which is also available in Google Maps. These concerns mainly focus on images showing people doing things that they may not wish to be publicized, such as men visiting strip clubs or picking up prostitutes. Perhaps more significant, critics expressed concern that the images could identify vulnerable areas such as shelters for victims of domestic violence or areas frequented by political dissidents.

## GOOGLE IN SPACE?

Page learned to fly helicopters, but Brin wants to fly even higher. In 2007, he paid a $5 million deposit for a future seat aboard a Russian *Soyuz* spacecraft, marketed by a company called Space Adventures. He hopes to visit the *International Space Station*, perhaps by 2012.

Meanwhile, by arrangement with the Geoeye satellite imaging company, Google now has its own Google-branded satellite circling the Earth, helping to provide better images for Google Maps and Google Earth.

In 2007, Google launched another space initiative. Until recently, nearly all space launches were funded and controlled by government agencies such as NASA. This contrasts with the early development of aviation, which featured a broader mix of public and private funding. While the military and the post office (through air mail contracts) played an important role in the development of bigger, faster, more reliable aircraft, private airlines had sprung up by the 1920s, only two decades after the Wright brothers had first taken to the air.

Originally created in 1996, by 2004 the Ansari X Prize offered $10 million for the first nongovernmental organization to launch a reusable

Google has maintained that its pictures only show public areas, and that people do not have an expectation of privacy when they are in public. However, critics have pointed out that Google's elevated cameras can view angles that would not be available to ordinary passers-by. In May 2010, Google admitted that its camera cars had also captured information (such as Web site addresses) as people browsed the Internet over their wireless connections.

As a result, authorities in a number of countries have launched investigations of Street View. In Australia, Minister for Communications Stephen Conroy called the capture of wireless information "the largest privacy breach in history across western democracies." The European Union has made a number of demands, including requiring Google to notify residents before their area is photographed and to keep photos no longer than six months.

Google's response to the outcry showed the difficulty that Googlers, from Page and Brin on down, have had in understanding and responding to such concerns. Sometimes, Google tries to alleviate concerns, such as by withdrawing images of battered women's shelters or blurring faces and car manned spacecraft twice within a two-week period, demonstrating the potential for a commercial "spaceline." In October 2004, the experimental craft *SpaceShipOne*, designed by Burt Rutan and financed by Microsoft cofounder Paul Allen, succeeded in meeting these conditions and received the prize.

In September 2007, Google announced that it was donating $20 million to the X Prize Foundation for the first private group to land a robot rover on the Moon's surface and return images and data. In a video announcing the prize, Brin said that Google was supporting this effort because it "is really going to accomplish something very, very impressive . . . something . . . only a couple of governments have ever accomplished."

Google has done other things to direct people's attention to the final frontier of space. In 2009, the 40th anniversary of the Apollo moon landing, Google announced that it had added views of the lunar surface (including Apollo landing sites) to its Google Earth product. For those wanting to look even farther afield, detailed imagery of Mars has also been added, taken from several recent Mars probes including the *Mars Reconnaissance Orbiter* and the *Mars Exploration Rovers (Spirit* and *Opportunity)*.

license plates. On the other hand, Google sometimes has decided to simply stop providing Street View imagery in some countries, including Australia and Germany.

Googlers wanted to offer the world a portrait of itself, but the world is made up of many cultures, each with its own views about privacy. For Google, the value of information can only be realized when it has the largest possible scope, but the process of negotiating conflicting interests has been difficult at best.

## ALL THE BOOKS IN THE WORLD

Just as adding maps and imagery provided a new dimension to Google's offerings, the company from its earliest years has also tried to expand the amount and kind of text that can be found online. Google may have started out as a high tech library catalog, but it soon wanted to put the library itself online.

In 2001, Page and Brin gave a joint talk to the Commonwealth Club of California in San Francisco. Page noted that as exciting as the Web and Internet were they had serious limitations:

> You can't access content that's in libraries. You can't access magazines. You can't access newspapers, in general, or old newspaper content. You can't access all the television programs that have ever been broadcast. But all these things will happen.

Vine and Malseed quote Page as having a personal interest as well: "I just wanted to be able to search libraries myself. You get interested in something and want to see the state of human knowledge."

Just as Page once had thought they could download the whole Web in a couple of weeks, the head Googlers might have underestimated how long it would take to put the world's books online. Nevertheless, by the end of 2003, Page and Brin were ready to announce Google Print (later called Google Books). The goal of this project was nothing less than to scan and make digitally accessible every book in existence, in print or out of print.

Marisa Mayer (1975–   ), now Google's vice president of location and local services, called this effort "our moon shot." Back in 1961, President John F. Kennedy had set America a goal of landing people on the moon in 10 years. Google set a goal to digitize at least 15 million books within a decade. (Google also announced another kind of moon shot in its 2004 April Fool's press release. It proclaimed the latest addition to the Googleplex, the Google Copernicus Center, also called the Googlunaplex. This moon-based research facility would deliver "entropized, information-filtering, high-density, high delivery hosting," abbreviated "HiDeHiDeHo.")

Since then Google has steadily expanded the project. The program received a hefty boost in December 2004 when Google signed an agreement with several top libraries (including Harvard, Stanford, Oxford, and the New York Public Library) to digitize their collections. Since then, a number of other prominent libraries have joined the project.

Even with special-purpose high-speed scanners and OCR (optical character recognition) software, the physical aspects of the task are daunting. Requiring a long-term effort with little prospect of immediate profit, Google Books is an example of how Page and Brin often put their vision of a vast universe of information ahead of practical considerations.

By 2009, Page was looking back on the progress of Google Books and on what could be found there:

I was amazed to see on Google Books a fully accessible archive of some priceless magazines, including *Popular Science*—going back 137 years! It has all the ads and everything, though they didn't seem to have many ads back in the April 1872 edition. It is truly a dream fulfilled for me that we now have 12 million books scanned and available for searching at books.google.com. That is already bigger than almost any university library, and we're not done yet

However, Google Books has also been cited as an example of how the two idealistic entrepreneurs can run roughshod over the interests of other groups of people. While books considered no longer to be in copyright (that is, in the public domain) present no problem, Google's policy toward copyrighted works was met with opposition from some publishers and authors' groups.

Google's intention was to make a limited amount of text from copyrighted books available, such as the cover, table of contents, and a limited number of excerpts matched to search terms. However, in 2005, the Authors Guild and the Association of American Publishers in separate lawsuits charged that Google was violating copyright law by using the text without permission. Google in turn argued that their program was covered by fair use, a part of copyright law that allowed use of limited excerpts of text for certain purposes such as scholarship.

In 2008, Google and the authors and publishers groups came to a legal settlement. Google agreed to pay $125 million to compensate people or companies whose copyrights had allegedly been infringed, as well as to pay their legal expenses. A complicated system was set up to share future revenues with authors and publishers.

However, the agreement raised further issues. Some critics charged that Google may still have too much control over how books are digitized and distributed, putting authors and publishers at a disadvantage. On March 22, 2011, U.S. Circuit Judge Denny Chin issued a ruling rejecting the settlement. Among other things, he urged that instead of requiring that authors "opt out" if they did not want their books in Google's system, Google be allowed to include only those books whose authors agree, or "opt in." Google opposes this because of the time and effort it would take to find and contact millions of authors and the likelihood that a substantial number of authors might not agree to have their books included. As of early 2012, the legal issue remains unresolved.

As with record labels, book publishers have been faced with new competition from online services that attempt to cut out the middleman (a process called *disintermediation*) and have the creators of intellectual property sell it directly to users. Some advocates of Internet freedom want to see an end to legal or technical restrictions against freely copying or distributing works. In Daniel Alef's book *The Gatekeepers,* Ken Auletta asks Brin about these issues:

> [Auletta] asked Sergey if he expected "authors to generate their income by selling advertising in their books. If there was no advance from a publisher, who would pay to cover the writer's travel expenses? . . ." He wanted to know "who would edit and copyedit the book," how authors would get paid, who would pay lawyers to vet it or hire people to market the book. Auletta noted that "The usually voluble Brin grew quiet, ready to change the subject."

Thus far we have seen many brick and mortar bookstores close under the competitive pressure of online booksellers, notably the giant Amazon. Handheld *e-reader* devices from Amazon, Barnes and Noble, and others are growing in popularity, and Amazon recently announced that it is now selling more *e-books* than printed paper books. Google, meanwhile, continues to extend its virtual library to include many newspapers and magazines from the 19th and early 20th centuries, providing researchers with new resources even while legal questions remain unresolved.

## GOOGLE TACKLES E-MAIL

Even as Google was offering new kinds of content to users, it was becoming more involved in how people communicate. By the early 2000s, e-mail had become an important part of peoples' lives, but it was accompanied by a considerable amount of frustration. Google had been quietly working on a Web-based e-mail system for internal use—it had started as an engineer's *20 percent time* project.

In March 2004, Google invited about 1,000 industry and opinion leaders to join Gmail—and invite their friends. (This controlled access testing of not-quite-finished software is known in the industry as a *beta test.*) Gradually, additional batches of people were invited to try the service (and to invite their friends.) As word about Gmail's features spread, invitations actually began to be sold on eBay, sometimes for hundreds of dollars!

A bit oddly, Google formally announced Gmail on April 1, 2004—April Fool's Day. While this might have caused some confusion, Gmail was quite real. In the press release, Page noted that he had received a message from an unhappy e-mail user:

> She kvetched [complained] about spending all her time filing messages or trying to find them. And when she's not doing that, she had to delete mail like crazy to stay under the obligatory four-megabyte limit. Can't you people fix this?

Brin then added his own thoughts: "If a Google user has a problem with e-mail, well, so do we."

Gmail had a number of attractive features. Since Google's philosophy was that storage was relatively cheap and would only get cheaper, Gmail offered a whole gigabyte (1 GB) of space for each user's mail. This meant that users did not have to worry about deleting old messages to save space. Further, keeping e-mail available indefinitely allowed for easy retrieval. Google's search technology was built in, so if a user remembered only a few words or phrases in an old e-mail, it could be retrieved by a quick search. Finally, using technology similar to that employed in matching keywords to ads, *spam* (unwanted, mass-distributed e-mail) was largely filtered out before it even reached the user's mailbox.

One Gmail feature was controversial, however. Google's sophisticated ad-matching software was used to display ads to the Gmail user based on keywords in the e-mail. Thus, if a user received a message from a friend talking about her vacation, a travel-related ad might appear. The ads were unobtrusive, but what bothered many people is that they meant that someone or something was reading their mail in order to display them. Traditionally, mail was about as private as anything could be—the government usually needs a court order to open someone's mail, after all.

Page and Brin were startled by this outburst of concern. As quoted by Vise and Malseed, Brin tried to reassure users:

> It sounded alarming but it isn't. The ads correlate to the message you're reading at the time. We're not keeping your mail and mining it or anything like that. And no information whatsoever goes out. We need to be protective of the mail and peoples' privacy. Any Web mail service will scan your e-mail. It scans it in order to show it to you; it scans it for spam. All we're doing is showing ads. It's automated. No one is looking.

These reassurances were not enough for many people. The scanning might be automatic and involve no actual human eyes, but people were beginning to realize just how much of their information passed through Google's hands. Google might be doing nothing wrong now but what about the future? Could they be trusted? How could a private company that was becoming so dominant in the world of online information be held accountable?

What was worse, the Gmail controversy arose just as Google was getting ready to sell its stock to the public for the first time. At most companies, a major and potentially controversial product would not be launched at such a sensitive time, but Google did not work that way. Google products began in the minds of freewheeling engineers, "percolated up" as they attracted interest within the company, and were often launched in stages, first as an experiment, then as a beta test, and finally as a fully backed product.

As concern grew, Page looked for a respected privacy advocate to advise him on how to make Gmail more privacy-friendly. He talked to Brad Templeton, a friend and chairman of the Electronic Frontier Foundation, a leading advocate for privacy and civil liberties in the online world.

A dialog began. Google had always been careful not to allow users' personal information to be sold or distributed to third parties. On the other hand, Google's technology depended on finding clever ways to use that information to tailor ads as well as its own services to the user's needs. But Templeton pointed out that despite Google's good intentions, having a vast and growing stock of user information was dangerous. In particular, governments could use legal means to compel Google to release information—for example, in an effort to prosecute dissenters. Further, he argued that users needed to be educated about the fact that e-mail was not like a letter sealed in an envelope and sent through the post office. It was more like a postcard that anyone could turn over and read. Templeton was impressed with Gmail's features and Google's intentions, but he urged caution. While the uproar over Gmail gradually faded, and the service now has more than 200 million users, the potential collision between Google's growing power and privacy concerns had only begun.

# Going Public

Computers and software are big, serious business—but the people who have come up with the ideas that led to the modern PC, the Internet, the Web, and social networking have often been playful in spirit and unconventional in lifestyle.

A visitor to the *Googleplex* (as the corporate headquarters is known) had better be alert—a pack of engineers might shoot by on roller blades in an impromptu hockey game, or a scooter might whiz by, or a beach ball might come bouncing along. Google's programmers and designers work long hours—this is no 9 to 5 job. But they also get to play quite a bit, because from their own experience Page and Brin knew that to work well, creative people also needed to be able to play.

Besides the gourmet meals mentioned earlier, Google also provides many of the necessities of daily life so employees do not have to waste time fighting traffic. Thus Googlers can get the wash (or their hair) done and even see a doctor or dentist—all without leaving the Googleplex. This environment has resulted in Google repeatedly being listed as one of the 100 best companies to work for by *Fortune* magazine.

## MANAGING INNOVATION

The growing number of well-cared-for Google employees were hard at work finding new ways to use the search engine and the information they were obtaining about users. Google kept on adding to its offerings. Google's search engine was now available in 26 languages. Google also kept adding capabilities. One of the most important was image search. After all, the Web was becoming a highly visual medium as well as a source of text. By identifying more than 250 million images and their accompanying text, Google's search engine was now able to return images that corresponded to a search word or phrase. But Page and Brin and the other top Googlers knew there were many other things to be found and used online.

In 2002, Google offered its first Google Programming Contest. Contestants received a database of 900,000 Web pages and were challenged to create an interesting way to work with that data. The winner received $10,000, a visit to the Googleplex, and, at Google's option, a chance for their program to be on the full Google database.

Around this time, Page and Brin's attitude toward innovation became evident in more systematic ways. In most companies, if one has a new idea one has to submit it and get official backing. At Google, programmers and designers were encouraged to use 20 percent of their work time to develop whatever ideas or projects appealed to them. Page and Brin still had the final say as to what would become an official Google product, but even those projects that were not adopted were viewed as learning experiences, not failures.

However, the high priority given to inspired engineering could lead to friction with employees in other departments, such as marketing. Douglas Edwards, hired as a marketing expert, concluded that Google's real directive was, "If you weren't an engineer, your first directive was to avoid impeding the progress of those who were."

Further, Edwards described Google as a "Don't talk. Do. kind of culture, which made communication about our technical achievements erratic." This lack of communication could mean that marketers did not really understand the significance of new product features, while engineers might not be aware of how users might react to them.

For his part, Brin gradually tried to provide investors and the public with a clearer understanding of how Google worked. In the 2004 annual letter to shareholders, Brin gave more details about how the company allocated its resources:

> We have decided that we need balance among core and expanded services. Larry and I use a rule called 70-20-10. Seventy percent of our effort goes to our core: our web search engine and our advertising network. These products still are the largest contributors to the financial health of the com-

pany. . . . But incremental resources have diminishing returns in almost any undertaking, so it is not desirable to put all your resources on the core product. That's why we allocate 20 percent for adjacent areas such as Gmail and Google Desktop Search. The remaining 10 percent is saved for anything else, giving us the freedom to innovate.

In the 2005 letter, Page described how Google developed many of its products from what start as experimental projects:

An important part of our development process is our willingness to experiment publicly. Our teams are more productive once they get real users and feedback. We have learned that the best way to make something great is to actually launch it to the public. That's why we have the Google Labs and "beta" labels—these are our experiments.

This balancing act between core products and freewheeling innovation constantly shifted as Page, Brin, and Schmidt tried to mediate between the need for revenue and the idealism and big dreams of the engineers.

The sometimes contradictory impulses in Google's culture were also reflected on a personal level, especially by Page. Page was known for being enthusiastic and generous when he believed someone had a good idea. As quoted by Brad Stone in *Bloomberg Businessweek* on January 26, 2011, Douglas Merrill, Google's chief information officer until 2008, believes that

Larry is a visionary, the kind of person that inspires people to do more, be better, reach farther. He would walk around the engineering department and, with just a word or two, guide or redirect projects and leave the developers feeling great about the coaching.

Page has often been described as an introvert who dislikes public speaking and prefers a quiet word or two. In the same article, Page suggests that rather than be upfront in the spotlight as CEO, he will encourage those who have already shown the strongest leadership: "We've been inspired by a lot of the people who have been operating with more autonomy and clear decision-making authority."

On the other hand, like many techies, Page can be brusque and dismissive if he did not think someone's idea was good. In general, for both Page and Brin, ideas, algorithms, data, and performance mattered—not avoiding hurt feelings.

## A NEW BUBBLE?

By the late 1990s, *dot-coms,* or Internet-based businesses, had become all the rage in the media and on Wall Street. The idea that many kinds of goods or services could be profitably sold online seemed to have been proven by a few astonishing successes—notably, Amazon and eBay. Amazon, starting as an online bookseller, has turned into a retailing giant that offers not only books, music, and videos but just about everything else that can be boxed and shipped.

Amazon's business philosophy differed from most conventional companies in that it was not concerned with near-term profitability. Amazon CEO Jeff Bezos told prospective investors not to expect profits for four or five years. He was confident that as millions of people experienced the convenience and reliability of buying things online, that growing customer base could be offered a variety of new products and services with the right combination of volume and profitability.

The other big *e-commerce* success story of the late 1990s was the auction service e-Bay. Unlike Amazon, eBay sold nothing itself. Instead, it brought sellers and buyers together through auctions and fixed-price sales. Ten years after it offered its stock to the public, eBay's revenues had

---

Outside observers who were used to conventional companies with a clearly defined hierarchy and job descriptions have often had trouble knowing what to make of Google. In a January 12, 2008, interview with the *Singapore Times,* Eric Schmidt described Google as a

> . . . group culture. There are almost no individual decisions. . . . The really major, major decisions about the company are made by the founders and me—three is better than two. But almost all big decisions are made in groups of 15 or 20, after a long discussion. . . . The other philosophy we try to adopt is that you don't go for consensus, you go for the best idea, which is different.

As for the role of the top executives, Page and Brin described it in their 2004 "Letter from the Founders" like this:

soared to almost $7.7 billion, with registered users now numbering in the hundreds of millions.

The early successes of Amazon and eBay suggested that if a company could establish itself as the online destination for buying a particular product or obtaining a service it could gain effective control of its market through what is called the *network effect*.

The idea of the network effect is that each user of a service adds a bit more value to the service as compared to any competitors. For example, as more people joined eBay, it soon made little sense to use a much smaller competitor, since it would have far fewer potential bidders to run up the price of one's item. (Thus, both Amazon and Yahoo originally had auction services but found themselves pushed into irrelevance by eBay.)

The problem was that for every Amazon or eBay there were hundreds of companies that had little more than an idea and a vague plan for how to turn it into a business.

After the collapse of the dot-com market shortly after the turn of the 21st century, many analysts and investors were leery of betting on Internet-based businesses. Too often they had been based upon business plans that did not seem to be well thought out. Google too had to deal with the atmosphere of skepticism.

We run Google as a triumvirate. Sergey and I have worked closely together for the last eight years, five at Google. Eric, our CEO, joined Google three years ago. The three of us run the company collaboratively with Sergey and me as presidents. The structure is unconventional, but we have worked successfully in this way.

On the one hand, the three top Googlers believe that their way of finding consensus among themselves has worked well. On the other hand, a former Google executive quoted by Ken Auletta criticized "micro management at the top," and said a prime example is that the founders and Schmidt, or their designees, "have to sign off on each hire." Thus, in some ways, despite it now being a very large corporation, Google sometimes seemed to be run more like a family business.

# INITIAL PUBLIC OFFERING

The year 2003 was a banner one for Google. By the end of the year, Google's index had reached about 6 billion pages and 800 million images. Google was named Brand of the Year by Brandchannel, a respected marketing analysis site, and Page and Brin were named Persons of the Week by ABC News.

Google's founders had misgivings about becoming a public company since it would subject them to a whole additional layer of complex regulations, as well as perhaps forcing them to be more conventional and cautious about future plans. However, Google had already grown so big that regulations would soon require it to report information pretty much as though it were already a public corporation. Given that, it made increasing sense to accept the responsibilities of public ownership in return for the opportunity to raise substantially greater amounts of investment capital.

In their official filing for their *initial public offering* (IPO) Page and Brin declared, "Google is not a conventional company. We do not intend to become one . . . We have managed Google differently. We have also emphasized an atmosphere of creativity and challenge."

Their letter went on to state their company's objectives:

Sergey and I founded Google because we believed we could provide an important service to the world—instantly delivering relevant information on virtually any topic. Serving our end users is at the heart of what we do and remains our number one priority. Our goal is to develop services that significantly improve the lives of as many people as possible. In pursuing this goal, we may do things that we believe have a positive impact on the world, even if the near term financial returns are not obvious.

In effect, they warned investors not to look to Google for short-term profits and warned that they would not be bound by rigid market expectations. They noted that they tried to look not one quarter or one year ahead but three to five years. While this kind of long-term planning might be typical for a Japanese or European company, it was not the way American investors typically operated, especially in a hot tech market where, at least for awhile, dot-com companies had sprung up like weeds, only to wither into irrelevance just as quickly.

Page and Brin also explained why they were choosing a corporate structure in which each share of stock held by the founders and early employees would have 10 times the voting power of the shares to be sold to the public.

They argued that this would allow them independence and forestall potential takeovers by other companies that might seek to control Google simply to get access to its technology and revenues. They acknowledged that this structure was unusual in technology companies but had been used by newspaper and media companies to allow them to focus on delivering unbiased news rather than having to sacrifice their principles in favor of demands for short-term profits.

The two mathematically minded entrepreneurs could not resist a bit of humor in their IPO filing. One place on the form asks for the maximum amount of money they intended to raise. They gave the amount $2,718,281.828. These are the digits of the mathematical constant $e$ (2.718281828 . . .), the base for the exponential function, and found in everything from compound interest calculations to the more abstruse realms of calculus.

Perhaps, then, it is not surprising that Page and Brin would also choose an unconventional way to offer the stock to the public. The usual way to do an IPO is to select one or more investment bankers who, in exchange for a fee, set the price for the stock and offer it to their favored clients, who will stand to make a large profit if the stock price is driven up by popular interest. Smaller investors are left out of the loop.

The traditional process also pits the issuing company and the bank against each other: The bank wants to price the stock low enough to be sure to sell out (and earn its commission), while the company of course wants to sell the stock at the highest possible price in order to raise capital.

The Google founders decided to offer the stock through an auction process. Would-be investors could bid online for any amount of shares from five on up. A maximum price is set and progressively lowered until the clearing price is reached and all the shares have been spoken for. At that point, all bidders get the number of shares they bid for, paying that final price. Naturally, the investment banks were not happy at being largely cut out of the IPO process.

## BUMPS IN THE ROAD

Feeling energized about the future, Page and Brin found themselves giving an interview to David Sheff, an editor at *Playboy* magazine. Sheff begins his article with a colorful description of the two Google founders:

Both drive Priuses, Toyota's hybrid gas-and-electric car. It is impossible to imagine them in Brioni suits. Brin often wears a T-shirt and shorts. Page usually dresses in nondescript short-sleeve collared shirts. Both rent modest apartments. Their only indulgences so far fall into the realm of technology, such as Brin's Segway Human Transporter, which he occasionally rides around the Googleplex, the company's Silicon Valley headquarters. (Page often scoots around on Rollerblades or rides a bike.)

In response to a question about the Google motto, "Don't be evil," Brin replied, "We have tried to define precisely what it means to be a force for good—always do the right, ethical thing. Ultimately 'don't be evil' seems to be the easiest way to summarize it."

Sheff then asked them about how their IPO and future as a huge, public corporation might affect their ability to stay true to their motto. For example, accepting fees for better placement in search results could be quite profitable. A primary obligation of a public corporation is to maximize value—that is, make the most money—for its shareholders.

Brin deftly turned the question around. He asked Sheff why magazines such as *Playboy* kept advertisements separate from their regular articles. Sheff replied that journalism can only be credible if it is not influenced by advertisers. Page then smashed the metaphorical tennis ball back over the net: "There you go. It's no different for Google. People use Google because they trust us."

Answering a question about copyright (an issue that would cause endless Google-related controversies), Brin advocated for users getting as much information as possible. If something has to be removed for legal reasons, Google will include a notice explaining what has happened. The ultimate goal, according to Brin, was "to have the entire world's knowledge connected directly to your mind."

As deftly as Page and Brin had handled the interviewer's questions on the eve of their IPO, they had slipped up regarding timing. During the last few weeks before the stock is offered to the public, a company is supposed to observe a quiet period. Executives are not supposed to say anything that might encourage people to buy the stock or run up the price.

Page and Brin were told that the interview would appear in the September issue of *Playboy*—after the IPO. The only problem was that, as with most magazines, issues actually come out well before their cover date. The magazine came out in August, a week before the IPO. Faced with criticism, Page and Brin amended their IPO application, adding the interview as an appendix. This enabled them to say that it was part of the public record and avoided legal problems. After a week's delay, the IPO went ahead.

# LIFTOFF

On August 19, 2004, Page was invited to ring the opening bell at the NAS-DAQ stock exchange. Google stock opened at $85 per share and had risen to $100 by the end of the first day. Of the $1.67 billion raised, $1.2 billion was invested in the company and $473 million went to the Google executives and outside investors who sold their shares. Google was now a $27 billion company. In three months, the price of Google stock soared to $200 per share.

In August 2005 (a year after the original IPO), Google announced another stock offering of 14,159,265 shares. (Another sly mathematical reference, since the number pi is equal to 3.1415265.)

Selling this new stock would give Google a total of $7 billion in cash, which the company said it would use for "acquisitions of complementary businesses, technologies, and other assets."

In explaining to Vise and Malseed why Google needed more money to expand its range of services, Eric Schmidt referred to a concept known as the *long tail* of potential customers that it had been thought were unprofitable:

> The surprising thing about the Long Tail is how long the long part of the tail really is, and how many small businesses there are that have not [had access to] the mass market," Schmidt said. "We're doing pretty well in the middle of the tail. We still do not have all the products and services that in our judgment are really needed to serve the largest advertisers, or the very tiniest of advertisers. We want to make sure we serve this whole space very, very well, and that is all stuff under development.

# CASUAL BILLIONAIRES AND WEDDING PLANS

Page and Brin may have become billionaires, but their lifestyles did not change much. They still dressed casually most of the time and did not invest in mega mansions or yachts. When asked at Google's 2008 annual meeting whether anything was different for them, Brin admitted, "I have a pretty good toy budget now. I just got a new [computer] monitor." Page noted, "I don't have to do laundry."

They did buy a nice private jet, and in 2007 Brin and his girlfriend, Anne Wojcicki, put it to good use. Brin had met Anne through her sister Susan, the same Susan Wojcicki from whom Google had rented their garage office after leaving Stanford. When they agreed to get married, the couple invited their guests to join them aboard the jet, without telling them where they were going. The plane landed on a pristine island in the Bahamas, where Brin and Wojcicki (in black and white swimsuits respectively) exchanged vows.

In November 2007, it was the turn of Page and his girlfriend, Lucinda (Lucy) Southworth, to have their own secretly organized wedding, also on a Caribbean island.

Still only in their 30s, Page and Brin enjoy active sports and a bit of daring. Both enjoy kiteboarding, where surfboards are pulled rapidly through the water by parachute-like kites. (Brin has even built a kite-powered sailboat.)

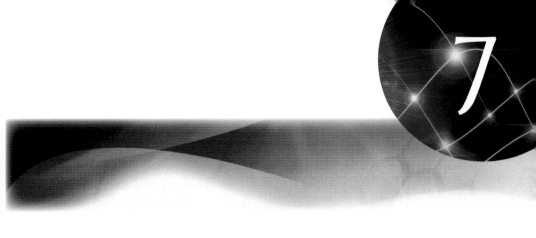

# Google in a Changing World

Just before Google's 2008 annual meeting, CEO Eric Schmidt emphasized that Page and Brin were fully capable of handling the challenges that were now facing what had become one of the world's greatest and most influential corporations. "The boys have grown up," Schmidt noted. "They now function in the company as senior executives with skills and experience." Page could then not resist interrupting, "We wish we had five years ago."

They would need all their skills and experience because Google's very success had brought it to center stage, subject to intense scrutiny by would-be competitors, analysts, activists, and, to an increasing extent, regulators. They would also have to deal with the worldwide financial crisis that began in 2008, triggered by a collapse in the U.S. real estate market. As Ken Auletta noted

> the new senior vice president and chief financial officer, Patrick Pichette, [is credited] "for forcing, for the first time, the company to focus on priorities" and to "allocate capital based on whether there are returns."

This did not mean that Google stopped innovating. Indeed, Google was moving toward becoming more of a media company as well as looking at new ways people were interacting with the Web. According to what Schmidt told Ken Auletta, even he continued to share the founder's idealism: "Our goal is to change the world. Making money is a technology to pay for it."

# YOUTUBE

One of the most important trends on the modern Web is a service that enables users not only to consume content (as in traditional television) but also to create and share their own text and videos. In February 2005, three former PayPal employees created YouTube as a way to enable users to share videos. (This was aided by the fact that inexpensive camcorders and, later, cell phones put some form of moviemaking in the hands of almost everyone.) After obtaining some venture capital, YouTube ran a beta test program for six months and then opened to the general public in November 2005. It was an instant success. Half a year later, YouTube announced that more than 65,000 new videos were being uploaded each day, and 100 million videos were being viewed daily.

In October 2006, Google announced that it had acquired YouTube in exchange for $1.65 billion in Google stock. In the conference call announcing the deal, Eric Schmidt declared, "This is the next step in the evolution of the Internet." Brin said, "It's hard to imagine a better fit with another company. This really reminds me of Google a few short years ago."

Certainly, the online delivery of videos, movies, and television programs has increased rapidly in the last few years. A recent trend is that more people are watching television on devices other than traditional television screens—often laptops and even cell phones. Using a process called *streaming,* a program can be downloaded from a server and watched simultaneously.

At the same time that television programs are showing up on computers, the Internet has been showing up on recent model televisions. Google has entered this market with Google TV. The system ties together Google's *Android* operating system and *Chrome* browser to create an interface that enables users to subscribe to and select television programs to be streamed to Internet-enabled TVs. However the new service has suffered from glitches and limited content due to the reluctance of cable TV networks and other providers to make their programs available. Stiff competition is also offered by other interactive television providers as well as Apple Computer, which offers its own television service.

YouTube has been successful in gaining a huge number of users, and it has also been influential socially and politically. Whether it is an embarrassing slip by a politician or video of protesters being attacked by tanks in the Middle East, YouTube now amounts to an alternative news channel.

However, with its new emphasis on sound business propositions, Google has had to face the problem of how to actually make money from YouTube users. According to Auletta, Schmidt announced that his "highest priority in 2008 was to figure out a way for YouTube to make money."

As a result, more kinds of advertising have been appearing on YouTube. Advertisers can pay to have videos promoted or featured at the top of listings. Some videos have a short ad that plays before the video starts. Sensitive to user frustration, Google has tried to make the advertising brief or unobtrusive. Of course, commercials that are truly interesting often get posted as YouTube videos, providing a sort of free advertising!

The debate continues as to the extent Google should obtain and provide its own content in addition to what users upload and share. Speaking to Ken Auletta, Page said that what Google should mainly do is:

> . . . aggregate content; we can process it, rank it, we can do lots of things that are valuable. We can build systems that let lots of people create content themselves. That's really where our leverage is.

In addition to video sharing through YouTube, Google provides photo sharing through Google Photos (formerly Picasa). Besides uploading, organizing, and sharing their photos, users can search for pictures by their content, thanks to sophisticated image-recognition software. However, as of 2011, this market was still dominated by Yahoo's very popular Flickr service. Of course, there are many other ways to share photos, such as through social networks such as Facebook or Google's own Google+. Indeed, the convergence of different ways to do things makes it hard to predict winners or losers on the Web of the 2010s.

## MOBILE REVOLUTION

What computer does the average person now use the most each day? Could it be a desktop computer, a laptop, or perhaps a *netbook*? No, the answer for an increasing number of people is the little computer in their pocket, a *smartphone*. Today's phones have faster processors and more memory than PCs had only a few years ago. Using operating systems such as Apple's iOS or Google's Android, the phones can run thousands of little programs or *apps* that can keep track of appointments, view or edit documents, or, of course, play games. By the end of 2010, shipments of smartphones had exceeded those of PCs for the first time. In 2011, 350,000 new phones running Android came online each day—not to mention thousands more from Apple, RIM (Blackberry), and others.

Google's mobile strategy, like most of the company's efforts, is complex and many faceted. Google purchased and has developed Android as an *open source* (freely available and modifiable) alternative to Apple's iOS. Indeed, Apple, until 2011 under charismatic and energetic CEO Steve Jobs (1955–2011) makes a good contrast to Google. While Google is decentralized and "lets a thousand flowers bloom" (even at the cost of some duds), Apple under Jobs's firm control crafted its products and user experience, with the aid of superb physical and user interface design.

Google's answer to Apple's controlled environment is to build a system based on open-source software. As Ken Auletta noted

> For Google, Android represented a perfect storm—its idealistic desire to promote an open, more democratic system meshed with its business interests. The more people who had access to the Internet, the more Google searches or Google Maps would be used, and the more data collected.

As of 2012, the outcome in the mobile market is far from clear. Because Android is freely available, Android phones are offered by dozens of manufacturers, while Apple offers one model, the iPhone. In terms of sheer numbers Android is now outselling Apple—though Apple makes much more money on each phone, since it sells the hardware itself.

Another important development is the arrival of the *tablet*—a slatelike computer such as Apple's very successful iPad. Although some Android-based tablets may be as good as (if not better) than the iPad in some respects, Apple's head start and huge number of apps seem to have kept Android tablets from really catching on.

Fortunately for Google, its strength is not in hardware but in the analysis and distribution of information. Thanks to the ability of services such as Google Maps and local search to give users relevant information (such as nearby businesses and transportation) as they travel, it does not matter that much whose device they are using—so long as they turn to Google for what they need. Auletta noted that by spring 2008:

> Google was buoyant. Rejecting the one-trick pony charge, Schmidt said that with mobile phones, plus search, plus its array of software products, and YouTube, he explained why it was conceivable that Google could become the first media company to generate one hundred billion dollars in revenues.

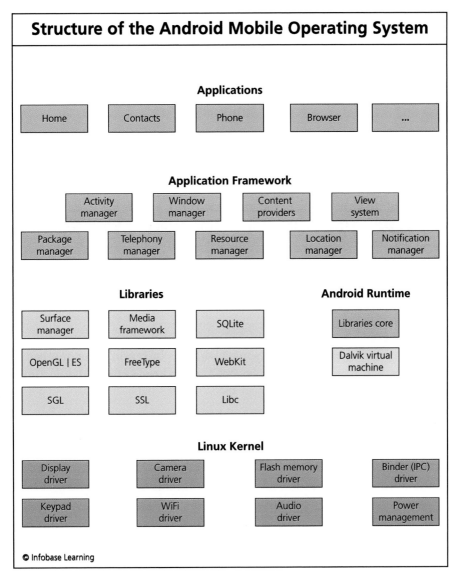

Structure of the Android Mobile Operating System

Based on the open source Linux operating system, Google's Android is becoming the most widely used OS for smart phones, as well as making some inroads into the tablet market. Android provides a variety of services and modules that can be called upon by application (app) developers.

In August 2011, however, Google made a move to the hardware side of the mobile market. The company announced it would acquire Motorola Mobility for $12.5 billion. If approved by Motorola shareholders and regulators, the deal would give Google its own hardware platforms, including the Droid X smartphone and the Xoom tablet.

However, the primary goal of the acquisition, according to industry observers, is not a desire by Google to expand into hardware manufacturing. Rather, it is to provide Google with an extensive new portfolio of patents to use in legal negotiations. Today's complex technology often involves a tangle of patent claims and counterclaims—a situation that has been decried by Page and Brin, among others, as stifling innovation and competition.

By 2011, Google's Android operating system had come under numerous patent challenges, sometimes settled by manufacturers agreeing to pay to license patents, particularly from Microsoft. With Motorola's mobile technology patents in hand, Google would be in a stronger position in its ongoing patent disputes with Apple and Microsoft, which have charged that Android violates their patents. This is because Google might now be able to claim that its competitors are violating the patents it has acquired. The battle of claims and counterclaims could then result in a settlement that all the companies can live with.

## UP IN THE CLOUD

The tech world often seems to resonate with one buzzword after another. A few years ago it was Web 2.0. In 2012, the phrase of the day is *cloud computing.*

The traditional way to deliver and use software is for people to buy the program on a CD (or perhaps download it) and run it on a desktop or laptop computer. Data such as word processing documents, spreadsheets, or photos would also be stored on individual computers. As a result, each user or organization would be responsible for keeping programs up to date and data safe.

Along with other giants such as Amazon, Google has come to the conclusion that both programs and data should be stored on servers and provided to users regardless of where they are or what device they are using. Thus, someone might create a report on a desktop computer, revise it on a laptop while flying to a meeting, and even insert some last minute updates using a smartphone. If all the data is stored in the cloud (that is, on Google's network of servers), every document will always be up to date. By providing multiple backups and redundancy, data would be protected so a business need not worry about making daily backups.

Although it cannot do everything that traditional office software such as that from Microsoft can do, Google's office software, called *Google Docs,* offers basic functions for word processing, spreadsheets, and presentations, plus some extras. In the long run, this software, as well as cloud-based and

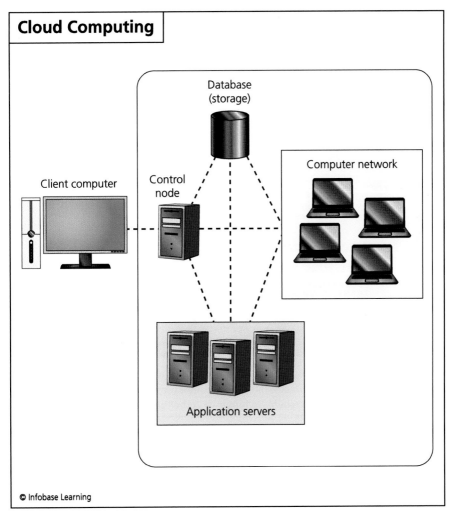

## Cloud Computing

Database (storage)

Computer network

Client computer

Control node

Application servers

© Infobase Learning

The storing of all documents as well as application programs online allows users to work anywhere on any device—as long as they can get an Internet connection. Cloud computing forms a major part of Google's corporate strategy and threatens traditional desktop operating systems such as Microsoft Windows.

free software from other companies, may be eroding Microsoft's revenues from its Office products.

The cloud idea also seems to fit the way people increasingly use computers. Most of their time seems to be spent visiting Web sites, searching and browsing, or sharing data and ideas through social networks such as *Facebook* and *Twitter*. This led Google engineers to ask whether a traditional operating system such as Windows was really needed by most users.

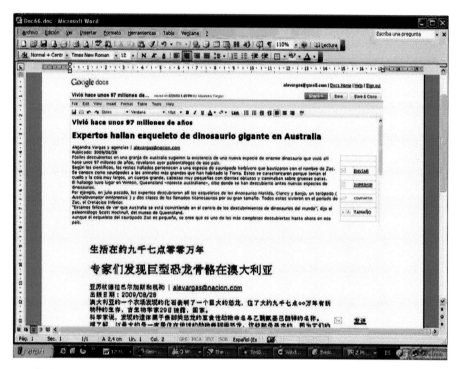

Google docs allow for the creation, editing, and sharing of documents in many languages—here, Spanish and Mandarin Chinese. Documents are compatible with Microsoft Word and other leading programs. *(Alejandra Vargas M./La Nacion de Costa Rica/Newscom)*

In 2011, Google offered the first laptop or netbook computers that run *Chrome OS.* Unlike an operating system such as Windows that provides elaborate ways to manage files and control the computer, users of Chrome OS do everything using a special version of the Chrome browser. Generally, reviewers of early versions of Chrome OS have noted that it is not yet capable of doing everything people are used to doing on a regular PC, since they are limited to only what can be managed or controlled through the Web.

The promise of cloud computing also raises questions that tie into other issues involving Google. Can one trust Google to keep one's data secure and private? What happens if one can't get an Internet connection? On February 24, 2009, Gmail's service halted for more than three hours.

## SOCIAL STUMBLES

In a sense, Google's services have always gained much of their power from social networks. After all, the original PageRank system evaluated the relevance of Web sites based on how Web site owners "voted" by linking to them. Through its acquisition of sites such as Blogger and particularly YouTube, Google has tapped into the willingness of people to create and share their writing and videos online.

In recent years, however, a powerful new platform has emerged: social networks such as Twitter and Facebook. Founded by Mark Zuckerberg (1984–   ) and his college friends in 2003, Facebook, much like Google, soon outgrew campus facilities. Also like Google, Facebook has had impressive and sustained growth, with 100 million users by 2008 and 750 million by 2011.

Just as Google has used its key asset (an excellent search engine) to expand into many other kinds of services and applications, Facebook has turned its social network into a platform for applications, including photo album sharing, blogs, and popular games such as Farmville.

Although Facebook is one of the biggest success stories of the Web, Twitter has perhaps gained an even more impressive presence in the online world. Developed in 2006 by Jack Dorsey, the Twitter service is basically simple. Drawing on the widespread adoption of texting (particularly by younger people), Twitter lets users send short text messages called tweets. The social networking aspect is that users can tune into other users' message streams by "following" them. By 2011, Twitter users were generating more than 200 million tweets per day. By that time streams of tweets by respected users had often become the most immediate source of breaking news during times of natural disaster or civil unrest.

Caught between the vast, sprawling platform of Facebook and the ease and flexibility of Twitter, Google's own social networking efforts proved to be an uphill climb. Google released its own social network site, Google Buzz, in February 2010. The service attempted to tie together a number of existing Google services, building upon its popular Gmail with blogging, photo sharing with its Picasa program, and YouTube. Google hoped that its ability to search for and manage data would make Buzz more attractive than the more sprawling, less integrated Facebook. At a press conference, Brin said that Buzz would also provide users with a service that would be equally useful at work and for leisure time, saying that "Bridging these two worlds is very powerful."

Buzz ran into a number of problems, however. As with Facebook, privacy concerns were raised. By default, Buzz made public information about a user's most frequently used Gmail contacts. The online privacy group EPIC filed a complaint with the Federal Trade Commission (FTC), alleging that Google Buzz "violated user expectations, diminished user privacy, contradicted Google's privacy policy, and may have violated federal wiretap laws." On February 16, 2010, another advocacy group, the Electronic Frontier Foundation, argued that

## CYBERBULLYING: WHO SHOULD BE RESPONSIBLE?

A tricky issue for Google and other providers of social networks and content-sharing sites arises when users post text or videos that defame or harass another person. For example, suppose a teenager breaks up with his girlfriend, then posts videos showing her undressed? Or suppose a video posted on a Facebook page singles out a student for harassment, perhaps because he is gay?

In general, under a section of the Federal Communications Decency Act, "no provider or user of an interactive computer service shall be treated as the publisher or speaker of any information provided by another information content provider." What this means is that if Google posts a news article or allows a blogger or YouTube user to post content, it is the author or poster who can be held liable for defamation (damage to someone's reputation) or other harm caused by the content.

As an international corporation, however, Google has sometimes run afoul of laws in other countries that are more protective of individual privacy. Thus, in 2010, an Italian court found three Google executives to be criminally liable for not removing a video in which a disabled boy was taunted by his classmates. The executives received suspended sentences, and Google protested that

> Common sense dictates that only the person who films and uploads a video to a hosting platform (such as Google) could take the steps necessary to protect the privacy and obtain the consent of the people they are filming.

In recent years, there has been growing concern about *cyberbullying* or the threatening or harassing of people (often vulnerable teenagers) in online chat rooms or social media. In a few cases, such bullying has even led to suicide. Again, this raises the question of what responsibility companies such as Google or Facebook should have for what Page and Brin would admit to be a serious social problem.

These problems arose because Google attempted to overcome its market disadvantage in competing with Twitter and Facebook by making a secondary use of your information. Google leveraged information gathered in a popular service (Gmail) with a new service (Buzz), and set a default to sharing your email contacts to maximize uptake of the service. In the process, the privacy of Google users was overlooked and ultimately compromised.

Google settled a class action lawsuit by agreeing to create an $8.5 million fund to promote privacy education for Web users. The FTC agreed with EPIC's complaint about Google's privacy practices and proposed a settlement that "bars the company from future privacy misrepresentations, requires it to implement a comprehensive privacy program, and calls for regular, independent privacy audits for the next 20 years."

As reporter Miguel Helft noted in the *New York Times* on February 12, 2010, "Google is known for releasing new products before they are fully ready and then improving them over time." While this practice has given Google a real advantage over competitors in harnessing creativity and responding rapidly to the changing world of the Internet, it has also caused some embarrassing stumbles. Google Buzz never really caught on nor challenged the domination of Facebook. (The service was discontinued in 2011.)

## GOOGLE FINALLY GETS SOCIAL?

Stumble or not, Google's practice of letting projects bubble up from the labs and get released as beta (test) versions means that the company always has another chance to get something right. As of 2011, the latest Google foray into social networking is called the *Google+* project. In a June 28, 2011, article in the Search Engine Land Web site, Vic Gundotra, Google vice president in charge of social products, says, "It's Plus because it takes products from Google and makes them better and project because it's an ongoing set of products."

In the same article, Google seems a bit coy when asked whether Google+ is a new attempt to compete with Facebook:

No. We realize that today people are increasingly connecting with one another on the web. But the ways in which we connect online are limited and don't mimic our real-life relationships. The Google+ project is our attempt to make online sharing even better. We aren't trying to replace what's currently available, we just want to introduce a new way to connect online with the people that matter to you.

Whatever caution Google might be expressing, the media immediately filled with stories suggesting an impending collision between two of the Web's biggest success stories. The reaction to Google+ has been considerably more favorable than it was for Buzz. For one thing, Google seems to have taken the earlier privacy concerns to heart: Postings are treated as private by default, and settings are clearer and easier to use than has been the case with Facebook. Google+ lets users set up specific circles of friends and control which group can see which posting. The screens the user sees are also less cluttered, in keeping with Google's tendency toward minimalism. Only two weeks after its launch, Google+ already had 10 million users. (By September 2011 the user base had grown to more than 40 million.)

During the company's second quarter 2011 earnings report Webcast for investors, Page noted that

> Our goal with Google Plus is to make sharing on the Web like sharing in real life, as well as to improve the overall Google experience. Circles lets you choose with precision who you're sharing with. Not surprisingly, this has been very well received, because in real life we share different things with different people. Hangouts allows for serendipitous interactions, like in real life when you run into a few friends. It gives you seamless and fun multi-user video, and it is really amazing. Last quarter we launched the +1 button in search results and ads, enabling users to recommend stuff they like and to have those recommendations show up in the search results of people they know.

The big challenge for Google, Facebook, Twitter, and other social networking companies is to find a way to actually make money from what their users do online. Google has been quite successful in learning about its users' interests and targeting ads to them. However, as Bob Garfield points out in an article for IEEE spectrum in June 2011, the effectiveness of standard ads is limited. Put simply, people do not like to be interrupted and usually will not click on ads that are displayed across the top of the screen or worse, that pop up in the middle of what they are reading. On the other hand, Garfield also notes that

> there is also the ability to target friends of existing customers—what venture capitalist David Pakman calls "the most powerful form of advertising ever created, not counting search." Not only is such targeted advertising on average twice as lucrative as conventional ads, it can fetch 100 times as much revenue as mere spam.

Further, Google has the great advantage that it has many successful systems that can feed users into their latest efforts. Social plus local may be an irresistible combination. Writing for the June 2011 issue of *IEEE Spectrum,* Elise Ackerman and Erico Guizzo point out that

> Most of the time when you use your phone, you're immersed in a specific context: There's the location, the day and time, what you're doing there, what is nearby, whether you've been there before. There's also your social graph—the connections among individuals, as well as among individuals and objects—with bits of data that are relevant to that context (whether, say, any friends have shared information about that location). The future of mobile computing will be all about how big companies and start-ups alike develop technologies—data analytics and machine learning algorithms, for example—capable of making sense of context data to provide better search results, advertising, and other services.

Thus in its repeated efforts to get social networking, right, Google has shown adaptability and resilience as it entered the second decade of the 21st century. However, Google's very success in dominating many aspects of online life has raised the concerns of civil libertarians, privacy, and consumer advocates.

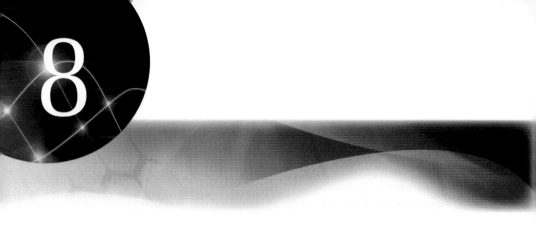

# Power and Responsibility

In the years since it went public, Google has become for many people their gateway to the Internet, shaping how information is found, evaluated, and used. Google's commanding market position shapes the world of online advertising. The company's widely used applications such as Gmail and the new social network Google+ shape the daily communications and relationships of millions of users.

Google's power gives rise to inevitable issues. Is Google too powerful? Should a private corporation be allowed to have such a dominant position in the online world? What government regulations, if any, are needed? Nor surprisingly, Page, Brin, and other prominent Googlers have their own strong opinions on these issues.

## DOING GOOD

Almost since its start, Page and Brin held that the purpose of Google was more than to achieve business success. Certainly, they believed that making the world's information freely accessible to all would empower individuals and groups (including activists) to work for more freedom and better living conditions for all. But they also were looking for ways that Google could use part of the money it had earned to fund worthy projects directly.

In 1994, Microsoft's Bill Gates (1955–   ) and his wife, Melinda, and father, William H. Gates, Sr., formed a charitable foundation. Today, renamed the Bill & Melinda Gates Foundation, the institution has an endowment of more than $34 billion. Its efforts range from developing financial institutions for the poor to agricultural reform, education, and health care initiatives (including vaccination and HIV/AIDs research).

Perhaps inspired by this lead, Page and Brin formed Google.org as the company's philanthropic arm. At the time of Google's IPO, Google.org was granted 3 million shares that today are worth approximately $1.8 billion. Google also donates 1 percent of its annual profits to Google.org.

In the 2005 annual letter, Page talked about the foundation and how they found the person to lead it.

> We searched far and wide for the unique leader who we thought embodies this goal in spirit and accomplishments, and we've found that person in Dr. Larry Brilliant. Larry was one of the key leaders in the global eradication of smallpox, living in India for many years. He was also chief executive officer of two public companies, was a professor at the University of Michigan, is a medical doctor, and cofounded both the early legendary online community the Well and the Seva Foundation for global development and health. While we were searching for Larry, we set up and funded the Google Foundation and refined its focus areas to providing sustainable development for the world's poorest citizens and harnessing people, money, and scientific resources to combat climate change. We have already provided funding of $7 million to Acumen Fund and TechnoServe, organizations that are taking unique approaches to solving these tough issues.

Google.org's focus is somewhat different from that of the larger Gates Foundation. Its main efforts in recent years have been in the area of renewable energy. In November 2007, the foundation announced the rather cryptically named RE<C meaning "renewable energy cheaper than coal." Focusing on both wind and solar sources, the project's goal is to generate at least 1 gigawatt (billion watts) of energy, enough to power a large city, at a cost less than that of producing it from coal.

Google's approach to philanthropy is also a little different in that it combines financial donations with donation of the time and expertise of the many scientists and engineers who work at Google. Using this approach, called hybrid philanthropy, Google might, for example, not only invest in alternate energy systems, but develop software and systems to link energy users to sources and even to create a smarter energy grid to distribute power.

# THE CHINA DILEMMA

Using Google's technology to help build a better future is one thing. A more difficult question for Google has been how to deal with the issues arising from the very technology that has made the company so successful. One such issue involves government censorship and its effect on the ability of users to gain access to Google's services.

In terms of population, economic growth, and Internet use, Asia in general is booming—and China in particular is the world's fastest growing large economy. Like other Western companies, Google has faced challenges in understanding China's culture and economic system. But as a provider of online links and information, Google has faced the additional challenge of censorship.

Google began operating a Chinese-language version of its search engine in 2002. Two years later, it brought out a Chinese version of Google news. China, however, has a longstanding policy of restricting citizens' access to information that it deems politically sensitive, such as stories about antigovernment protests or corrupt officials.

Page, Brin, and other Googlers were faced with a dilemma. They did not want to censor information—Google's stated purpose, after all, was to provide the greatest amount of useful information to people. Thanks to China's economic progress, millions of Chinese citizens now had the ability to go online and were eager to connect to the world in search of ideas and economic opportunities. But the Chinese government, using an Internet filter dubbed the "Great Firewall," frequently blocked access to Google's sites from within China.

During 2006, Page, Brin, and Schmidt debated what to do about the China situation. As quoted by Vise and Malseed, Schmidt said, "We actually did an evil scale." By this he meant they tried to determine what would be less harmful—sticking to their no-censorship policy and risking being cut completely off from China or agreeing to remove sites the Chinese government deemed to be offensive. In that case, Chinese citizens would at least still have access to the many other sites and services Google could offer—and, not incidentally, Google would have access to the rapidly growing Chinese market and the ability to sell advertising there.

Google decided that operating under Chinese rules was the lesser evil, so in October 2006 they set up a separate site, Google.cn. Users accessing the site would have certain search results censored, but in keeping with what it calls its transparency policy, Google would tell users when it blocked results.

Google also resisted attempts by the Chinese government to obtain information about users that it suspected of being dissidents.

Brin particularly was not happy with this compromise. After all, he had grown up in the repressive world of the Soviet Union. A number of outspoken online advocates were not happy with Google's decision either. Two sayings common among the architects of the Internet are "information wants to be free" and "the Internet views censorship as a failure and routes around it." For many, censorship is the very opposite of how the Web is supposed to work.

Meanwhile, at the start of 2010, Google reported that unknown people in China (who many Googlers suspected were working within the Chinese government) had attempted to crack Google's Gmail system and obtain personal information about Chinese citizens and others suspected of being dissidents or human rights advocates. Google said that it had had enough and would no longer submit its search results to Chinese censorship.

Government censorship, particularly in China, has posed a dilemma for Google's efforts to make the world's information fully accessible. Here, activists in Hong Kong unfurl a banner that reads "Say no to Internet censorship. Well done Google." (*Jerome Favre/Bloomberg via Getty Images*)

Google held out hope that the Chinese might come to a new compromise and stop such attacks. Brin told the *Los Angeles Times* in March 2010, "Our focus has really been what's best for the Chinese people. It's not been about our revenue and profit."

When negotiation with Chinese officials failed to reach an agreement, Google began rerouting search requests from Google.cn to a site in Hong Kong. (When the former British colony of Hong Kong became part of China, it was agreed that it could keep laws that provided for a greater degree of freedom than that allowed on the mainland.)

In making the announcement, Brin declared that

> I think at some point it is appropriate to stand up for your principles, and if more companies, governments, and individuals did that, I think the world would be a better place.

China responded by blocking access to all Google search sites from the mainland. Access to other Google services such as e-mail was not affected, but that threat remained, as well as the threat to withdraw Google's license to operate in China at all. Google backed off, removing the automatic redirect to Hong Kong, and making it a simple link instead—a link that China could block at will. In effect, censorship continues, although technically minded users have ways of getting around it by going through a third site called a proxy.

In general, the Chinese market has proven disappointing for Google in monetary terms. As of early 2012, China's homegrown Baidu search engine had about a 79 percent market share while Google trailed far behind at only 17 percent.

While China gets the most attention in the debate over Internet censorship, a number of countries in fact control access to Web sites and sometimes attempt to block the Internet entirely.

Speaking at a conference in Ireland in June 2011, Eric Schmidt warned that as authoritarian governments have learned about how effective the Internet can be for organizing dissidents (as in the Arab Spring in Egypt, Yemen, Tunisia, and other countries in early 2011), more censorship is likely.

> The reason is that as the technology becomes more pervasive and as the citizenry becomes completely wired and the content gets localised [sic] to the language of the country, it becomes an issue like television.

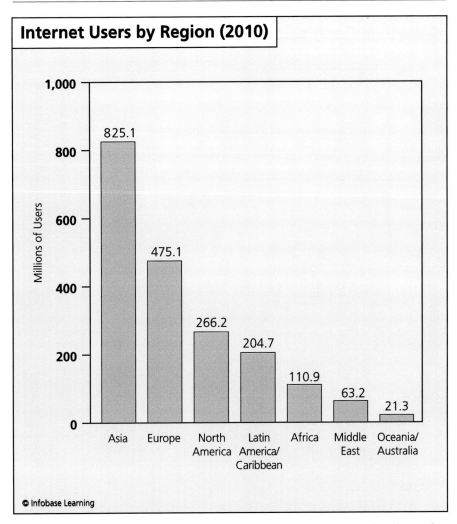

## Internet Users by Region (2010)

Millions of Users

- Asia: 825.1
- Europe: 475.1
- North America: 266.2
- Latin America/Caribbean: 204.7
- Africa: 110.9
- Middle East: 63.2
- Oceania/Australia: 21.3

© Infobase Learning

With Asia now having more Internet users than Europe and North America combined, it can be seen why Google's choice to enter or leave the Chinese market is a difficult one.

If you look at television in most of these countries, television is highly regulated because the leaders, partial dictators, half dictators or whatever you want to call them understand the power of television imagery to keep their citizenry in some bucket.

Government censorship is not the only potential threat to the free flow of, and access to, information on the Internet. A major debate in recent years has been over the principle of *net neutrality*. Net neutrality refers to the

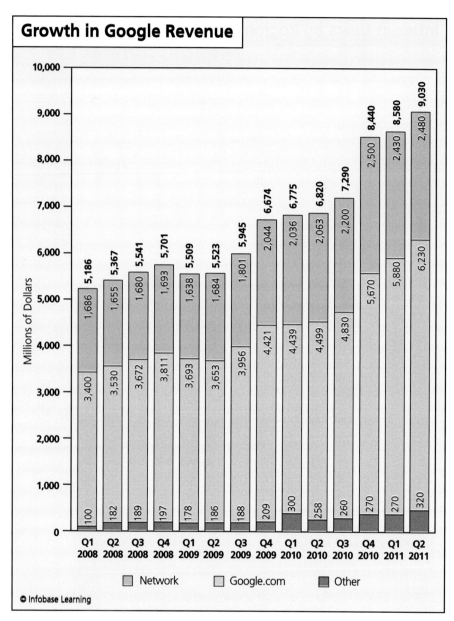

## Growth in Google Revenue

From 2008–10, Google's annual revenue grew by about 25 percent. However Google's dominant position in the search market has raised concerns about monopoly power.

principle that neither governments nor private service providers should be allowed to treat different types of content, users, or platforms differently. Some service providers have sought to slow down some kinds of data transmission (such as peer-to-peer file sharing services) or charge more for other services (such as streaming movies). Providers have argued that they need the right to slow down or "throttle" traffic in some cases because the demand for data is outstripping the capacity they can provide on their networks. They also may want a share of the revenue for premium content.

At first Google staked out a position solidly in favor of net neutrality— that is, opposing any form of content-based discrimination on either wired or wireless networks. However, in August 2010, Google and Verizon agreed on a modified position: Users should be free to access any content or service that is not illegal, using any device that was compatible with and did not harm the network. However, they also agreed that wireless service providers could throttle transmissions on the basis of content. Many advocates of net neutrality viewed this as virtually a sell-out by Google, but defenders of the policy suggest that without such controls, wireless networks (such as those provided by Verizon, AT&T, and T-Mobile) would be in danger of being overwhelmed, degrading service for all users.

## VANISHING PRIVACY?

As was seen with programs such as Gmail and Street View, new Google products have often raised privacy issues. Google's business model depends on getting as much detailed information about users as possible, in order to be able to better target ads to them. This information, obtained with the aid of small files called *cookies,* can include a history of the user's Web browsing, including what has been clicked on and even how much time was spent there. Similarly, Google's collecting of information sent over users' wireless networks was motivated by a desire to make maps and navigation more accurate, particularly for devices not equipped with GPS. (A similar issue arose in 2011 in connection with Apple collecting location information from iPhone users, sufficient to provide a fairly accurate track of the user's movements over the past months.)

Typically, companies give users some form of notice about the information they gather and whether they share it with other companies. However, this information is often buried in lengthy statements in legalese that most people agree to without reading. In many cases, users have been dismayed or angered later when they learn via the media about the extent in which their information is being collected.

An early example of how Google debated how to handle this issue came in 2000, in connection with Google Toolbar, a feature that adds a search box and other functions to the user's *Web browser*. One toolbar feature gave the user the opportunity to see an indication of the PageRank score of the page currently being viewed. This might give the user some indication of how relevant Google thinks that page is to his or her search. However, the real value of this feature to Google is that in order to calculate this value, Google needed to know what sites the user had previously visited. This information could be used to target ads based on the user's browsing history.

Newly hired Google marketer Douglas Edwards was dubious about the proposed Google Toolbar:

> I thought it was an enormous privacy tradeoff. I knew we planned to ano-
> nymize [sic] the data and wouldn't match the list of visited sites to a user's
> identity. Still, it felt creepy to me and I figured I wouldn't be the only one.
> So how to inform users without scaring them off?

The toolbar installation would include the option to not include the PageRank feature, in which case the user browsing history information would not be collected. However, Google would want most users to agree to install the toolbar so that the information would be available. Edwards struggled to balance Google's desires and his own belief that users should know what they were potentially agreeing to do.

> The wording users saw when downloading the Google Toolbar had to be
> subtle and assuage their concerns while downplaying the risks.
>     PLEASE READ THIS CAREFULLY, I wrote on the first line in large
> bold red letters. On a separate line beneath it, also red and bolded, came
> the words IT'S NOT THE USUAL YADA YADA. The text that followed
> was equally subtle: By using the Advanced Features version of the Google
> Toolbar, you may be sending information about the sites you visit to
> Google.

Edwards expected his proposed language to be argued over within Google—was it too direct, too subtle, or just right? In fact, the language was accepted and became part of the toolbar installation process. As Edwards noted

> News organizations from CNET to *MIT Technology Review* to *USA Today*
> and the *Washington Post* referred to Google's disclosure language in arti-

## Some Google Services

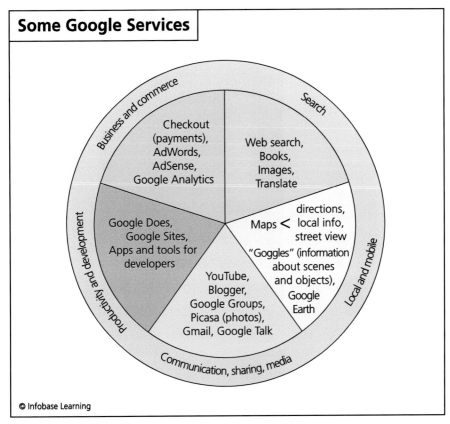

Business and commerce

Search

Checkout (payments), AdWords, AdSense, Google Analytics

Web search, Books, Images, Translate

Maps < directions, local info, street view

"Goggles" (information about scenes and objects), Google Earth

Local and mobile

Google Does, Google Sites, Apps and tools for developers

Productivity and development

YouTube, Blogger, Google Groups, Picasa (photos), Gmail, Google Talk

Communication, sharing, media

© Infobase Learning

Google has continually expanded search into new areas and has tailored results to the user's location. Advertising and a huge network of participating sites power Google's growth.

cles about the company and users' privacy, always giving Google the benefit of the doubt because it so clearly went out of its way to inform users about its intentions.

On the other hand, Ken Auletta quotes law professor Tim Lu about the ambivalence the Google founders seem to have toward privacy concerns:

"Google, if it were a person, has all the flaws and all of the virtues of a classic Silicon Valley geek," said Columbia's Tim Wu, who between jobs teaching law worked for a spell in the Valley. "In some ways, they are very principled." He cited Google's 20 percent time, saying that few "money-crazed companies would allow" such a thing. "But they have this total deaf

Getting Google's philosophy from the source—Larry Page at the Allen & Co. Media and Technology Conference in Sun Valley, Idaho, 2009 *(Matthew Staver/Landov)*

ear to certain types of issues. One of them is privacy." Why? Because, he said, "They just love that data because they can do neat things with it."

However, Auletta also quotes Page's perspective:

You don't want to do the wrong things in a way that is causing real damage to the world or to people. But you also need to make progress, and that's not always going to make everybody happy. The conflict between Google's desire to obtain more information that could make its services more useful and more valuable, and concern about possible misuse of that information, is not likely to go away.

# IS GOOGLE CHANGING OUR BRAIN?

In July 2011, a study by psychologist Betsy Sparrow of Columbia University published in the journal *Science* came to a remarkable conclusion. Search engines and online services such as Google and Yahoo are changing the way people remember things.

For many years, librarians and teachers have stressed to students that knowing how and where to find answers may be more important than memorizing facts that may or may not be needed later. Before the Web and search engines, finding facts when one needed them was often difficult or time-consuming. Looking up things in a printed encyclopedia or other reference book took time, and, in rapidly changing fields such as science and technology, the books were often out of date even before they were published.

Today's high school and college students can scarcely remember a time before Google and Wikipedia—or a time when newspapers and magazines were not online and had to be consulted in library stacks.

Sparrow and her research team found that if students are given a fact and told that it may be deleted from the computer later, they will make more effort to remember it. If, however, the students are confident the fact will be available from the computer indefinitely, they will tend to forget the fact itself. Instead they will remember how to retrieve it from the system.

There are several ways to look at this phenomenon. It could simply be a practical adaptation of the brain to what amounts to an extension of its own memory. Outsourcing the managing of facts to the computer might free human brains for doing the more creative things that (at least so far) computers cannot do well.

On the other hand, it is possible that people are becoming too dependent on technology to help them manage their lives. What happens if the technology fails? And if data stored in the computer begins to be treated as equivalent to personal memory, might too many facts be accepted without question?

Sparrow, on the other hand, suggests that relying on the computer to be responsible for storing knowledge might not be that different from the way people already rely on other people—such as specialists.

## GOVERNMENT INTRUSIONS?

Besides the potential for companies obtaining and misusing Web users' personal information for commercial purposes, there is also the fact that government agencies might want to obtain such information. Following the September 11, 2001, attacks, a reason often given is the need to identify and track potential terrorists. In subsequent years, there have been legal battles over whether, for example, telephone companies or Internet service providers should cooperate with government requests to obtain information about communications. (This is complicated by the fact that agencies can issue secret national security letters that prohibit anyone being informed about the interception, making legal action next to impossible.)

In the 2005 Google annual letter, Page argued that the company was willing to be proactive in protecting user privacy from what it viewed as overly aggressive government actions.

> The good news is that the interests of our company and those of our users are well aligned. If anything bad happens to you with respect to privacy, we could lose your trust, and that would hurt our business. Recently we received a subpoena from the U.S. government that was a broad request for URLs and user queries. We resisted the request in court and ultimately were asked to return only a small number of random URLs and no user queries. We will continue to work hard to protect our users' privacy, and think this ruling was a positive sign—a U.S. court siding with us in resisting overly broad requests for information.

On the other hand, Eric Schmidt, as quoted by Daniel Alef in *The Gatekeepers,* gave a much less reassuring statement.

> If you have something that you do not want anyone to know, maybe you shouldn't be doing it in the first place. If you really need that kind of privacy, the reality is that search engines—including Google—do retain this information for some time and it's important, for example, that we are all subject . . . to the Patriot Act, and it is possible that all that information could be made available to the authorities.

Since then, beliefs about Google's privacy policies have varied considerably. Sometimes, the company is praised for attempting to protect users against government intrusion, whether in China or in the United States. On the other hand, in 2007, the advocacy group Privacy International ranked Google as Hostile to Privacy, putting it at the bottom of its ranking of companies. In its report, the organization declared

> The view that Google "opens up" information through a range of attractive and advanced tools does not exempt the company from demonstrating responsible leadership in privacy. Google's increasing ability to deep-drill into the minutiae of a user's life and lifestyle choices must in our view be coupled with well defined and mature user controls and an equally mature privacy outlook. Neither of these elements has been demonstrated. Rather, we have witnessed an attitude to privacy within Google that at its most blatant is hostile, and at its most benign is ambivalent.

In response, longtime Google employee Matt Cutts, in a June 11, 2007, blog entry, questioned whether Google should really be ranked so low, charging that Privacy International seemed to ignore or gloss over AOL's releasing of millions of search queries and other companies turning over user information in response to government subpoenas rather than fighting them in court.

## TOO POWERFUL?

Google's sheer size and market power make issues such as privacy and the protection of intellectual property more important than they would be with smaller companies. Lance Ulanoff, writing for *PC Magazine* in 2007, said

> Google dominates all search queries. Period. . . . Recent statistics put the company's share of all Web searches at somewhere around 64 percent, with the total number of search queries growing by a massive 58 percent a year. These numbers have people wondering if [Google] is now a search monopoly.

(In 2011 Google's share of the search market was substantially the same.)

Back in 2003, Jonathan Zittrain of Harvard Law School described Page and Brin as "the traffic cop at the main intersection of the information society. . . . They have an awesome responsibility."

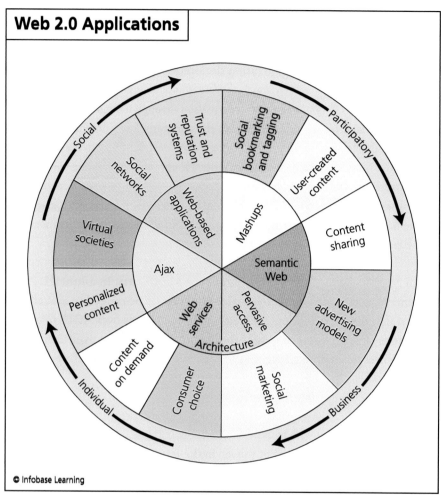

In its second decade of operation, Google is facing an online world in which the kinds of applications and the way people use them are changing. Important features include the direct streaming of media (music and video), social networking, and Web-based applications and services.

In addition to its domination of search, Google's ever-growing sources of content (such as YouTube, Blogger, and its new social network, Google+) may give it an unfair advantage in negotiating with content providers such as book publishers. (Similar complaints have been lodged against Amazon, which has brought book buyers lower prices at the expense perhaps of publishers' profits.)

Ken Auletta, who sees many admirable qualities in Google, nevertheless has noted that

Today, Google's software initiatives encroach on every media industry, from telephone to television to advertising to newspapers to magazines to book publishers to Hollywood studios to digital companies like Microsoft, Amazon, Apple, or eBay. For companies built on owning and selling or distributing that information, Google can be perceived as the new "Evil Empire."

The so-called old media (print publishers, newspapers, and magazines) have been struggling for more than a decade to adapt to a world in which most people want and expect to find their content online. The role of Google, a search company that has also become a major media company, is likely to remain complicated. After all, Google's products and services create much of the online environment that other companies must work within.

For their part, Page and Brin often seem to dismiss such concerns, perhaps believing that their overall good intentions will benefit consumers and, in the long run, content creators as well. In an October 15, 2003, Fireside Chat with Search Engine Watch, Brin insists that

Some say Google is God. Others say Google is Satan. But if they think Google is too powerful, remember that with search engines, unlike other companies, all it takes is a single click to go to another search engine. People come to Google because they choose to. We don't trick them.

At other times the chief Googlers, as quoted by Auletta suggest that one needs to be at least equally skeptical of the motives of the critics as the critics are of Google's motives.

Schmidt said he, Brin, and Page often ask themselves: "How can you grow big without doing evil?" He believes Google has become a lightning rod, particularly for old media. "In our society bigness is often associated with bad," he said. "There is no question that a company with the ambitions of Google will generate controversy, will have people upset with us. The question is: Where does it come from? Is it coming from a competitor? Is it coming from a business whose business model is being endangered by the Internet? Or is it because we're behaving badly?"

(continued on page 98)

## PERSONALIZED NEWS AND THE "FILTER BUBBLE"

On April Fool's Day in 2000, Google had announced MentalPlex, a new search engine feature that could read the user's mind in order to return the most accurate and relevant possible results. In effect, Google would know what the user was likely to want even before he or she had finished typing a query!

Fast forward about a decade, and in December 2009 a Google corporate blog made a quiet announcement. Starting that day it would provide "personalized search for everyone." Using 57 signals (indications such as the user's location, browser, and previous queries), Google would create a profile of the user and use it to predict what kinds of sites that person would like to see. What had been April foolishness had become reality.

Google's standard PageRank system also used many signals, but they were about the sites and their links, not the particular user who was doing a search. Theoretically, identical searches made at the same time by different users would return almost identical lists of results. But with this new system, each user would get a personalized, customized set of results.

This kind of customization extends beyond Google to news services, blog and feed readers, and other ways today's Web users obtain online content.

This kind of preselection is attractive to users. It offers people more of what they actually want, replacing time spent in fruitless searching or random browsing with the opportunity to read, view, or listen to things that are virtually guaranteed to be of interest. Of course, these new algorithms are attractive to search and content providers, because people will spend more time on their sites. Finally, for advertisers, it is the ultimate development of the technology that had started with matching search words to ads. Now both content and ads can be targeted and delivered before the user even asks for them!

Is there a downside to giving people what they want? Perhaps it is giving people *only* what the algorithm says they want. In his 2011 book *The Filter Bubble*, Eli Pariser, an Internet-savvy activist and journalist, gives an example of how Facebook had quietly reshaped his online experience.

My sense of unease crystallized when I noticed that my conservative friends had disappeared from my Facebook page. Politically, I lean to the left, but I like to hear what conservatives are thinking, and I've gone out of my way to befriend a few and add them as Facebook connections. I wanted to see what links they'd post, read their comments, and learn a bit from them. But their links never turned up in my Top News feed. Facebook was apparently doing the math and noticing that I was still clicking my progressive friends' links more than my conservative friends'—and links to the latest Lady Gaga videos more than either. So no conservative links for me.

Increasingly, Pariser argues that we will each be cocooned within a *filter bubble* that, unlike the heavy-handed censorship found in places such as China, is seamless and imperceptible.

This prospect raises questions about the future nature of our society. Back in the days when broadcast television was the main source of news for most people, everyone shared certain common experiences—the shocking assassinations of the 1960s, the Moon landing. In the cable and satellite era, television fragmented into hundreds of channels, but today new services are beginning to allow users to precisely determine what they will see—or have it determined for them, based on their interests.

Without a sense of shared experience, what happens to the possibility of political compromise and cooperation when people see only news and opinion that reinforces their existing beliefs? How can one think outside the box if one is no longer even aware that the box exists?

As Pariser puts it

Left to their own devices, personalization filters serve up a kind of invisible autopropaganda, indoctrinating us with our own ideas, amplifying our desire for things that are familiar and leaving us oblivious to the dangers lurking in the dark territory of the unknown.

Pariser offers a number of suggestions for breaking out of the filter bubble. He suggests *that people make a deliberate* effort to learn about

*(continues)*

*(continued)*

things that are off their usual track, whether politically or in terms of consumer choices. He also points out ways to reduce the ability of companies to track one's online habits, ranging from opting out of providing information to using incognito browsing features to simply choosing sites that "give users more control and visibility over how their filters work and how they use your personal information."

*(continued from page 95)*

Ultimately, when enough people are concerned about possible corporate abuses or misbehavior, legislators and government regulators are pressured to act. The problem is that the world of the Web is changing so rapidly that an attempt to fix one problem may become irrelevant in the light of later developments—or worse, cause more problems in turn. In the long run, it is society as a whole that must come to understand what new technologies and services offer and what risks come with them before sensible regulations can be devised. Individuals, too, need to be responsible for making choices and tradeoffs between, for example, the convenience of having one's online world tailored to one's wishes and needs and the danger of losing control over important personal information.

# Conclusion:
# Googling the Future

2011 seems to have opened a new chapter in the story of Page, Brin, and Google. In a press release the company announced the following:

- Starting from April 4, Larry Page, Google Co-Founder, will take charge of Google's day-to-day operations as Chief Executive Officer.
- Sergey Brin, Google Co-Founder, will devote his energy to strategic projects, in particular working on new products.
- Eric Schmidt will assume the role of Executive Chairman, focusing externally on deals, partnerships, customers and broader business relationships, government outreach and technology thought leadership—all of which are increasingly important given Google's global reach. Internally, he will continue to act as an advisor to Larry and Sergey.

In an article in *Search Engine Land,* Danny Sullivan suggested that the fact that Page had not been in the public arena for some time might help him (and Google) make a fresh start.

There's potentially a huge advantage in that, for Google. If Page is stepping up as the public face, it's an opportunity to defuse or put some of the gaffes associated with Schmidt behind the company. Page carries virtually no such baggage. That doesn't mean he gets a pass on anything associated with Google from before he took over. But it is a bit of a fresh start.

Later that year, Page and his team would make it clear that Google had not stopped innovating or expanding into new areas. The release of the Google+ service to the general public in September instantly created a major player in the social networking market. The pending acquisition of Motorola Mobile around the same time demonstrated Page's determination to defend Android from patent challenges. Meanwhile, the gradual introduction of netbook computers running the Web-based Chrome operating system will challenge the dominance of traditional desktop operating systems such as Microsoft Windows.

## NEW CHALLENGES

At the same time that Google was restructuring its top management, major challenges were looming. The FTC was investigating allegations that Google was using its dominance of the search market to gain an unfair advantage over competitors, such as by steering searchers to Google services. (A similar investigation by the European Commission (EC) was already underway, as well as an antitrust complaint filed by Microsoft, which has faced similar charges in the past over its Windows operating system.)

Meanwhile the settlement of the copyright charges involving the Google Books program was rejected by the court, leaving the future of the massive digital library project uncertain.

The *San Francisco Chronicle* writer James Temple suggested in April 2011 that Page may not be temperamentally suited to a task that involves skill in public relations and sensitivity to public opinion.

> . . . it's no secret that Page has a deep aversion to dealing with the news media and lacks the grace and polish that tend to come standard in Fortune 500 CEOs. By various accounts, Page can be awkward, aloof and dismissive of those who don't see the world in the unique way that he does.

Temple quotes analyst Rob Enderle

> A CEO has to be the public face of the company, and [Page] doesn't seem to want that. But he has to do that job. Right now, Google has a horrible public image, and he's got to fix that.

These concerns actually reflect a cultural difference between the world that developed computer geeks, technical innovators, and visionaries . . . and the world of politics, negotiation, compromise, and public perception. Page has passionately spoken of a world in which people are empowered by technology and information. He has insisted that everything Google does ultimately serves the consumer, even while benefiting advertisers and the company's bottom line. Like other innovators, Page and Brin seem genuinely baffled by many of the concerns about privacy and property rights. They see litigators and regulators as representing interests that are stubbornly holding back people from the limitless future promised by technology.

From the other side, the culture that grew up among programmers and inventors in Silicon Valley often seems naive, clueless, and even arrogant. Temple quotes author Siva Vaidhyanathan, author of *The Googlization of Everything.*

> I think that with Larry Page taking over Google, it's going to be more arrogance and more idealism, at the very moment when he should be humble and realistic, in order to get through these very real regulatory pressures.

Over the years, Google's pendulum has swung somewhat between open-ended innovation and a more practical focus on core products. The latest swing seems to be in the latter direction. In July 2011, while announcing Google's record quarterly earnings, Page said that he is pushing for more focus on products that are related to Google's core business as a search provider. He described this as "putting more wood behind fewer arrows."

Page then went on to say that Google Labs would be closed. Google Labs had been a sort of project incubator that seemed to typify the original spirit of Google as letting people try lots of things and then cultivating the most promising products. Some product-specific labs (such as Gmail Labs and Maps Labs) were to continue, but the fate of many other projects was not clear.

Page seemed to want to reassure stockholders that in an era of tight economics Google would be more cautious.

> "It is easy to focus on things we do that are speculative (e.g., driverless cars) but we spend the vast majority of our resources on the core products," Page

said to reassure investors. "We may have a few small speculative projects happening at any given time, but we're very careful stewards of shareholder money—we're not betting the farm on this stuff."

Continuing the practical note, Page said that Google wanted to create products and services that would be used around the world as part of peoples' daily lives, "just like a toothbrush."

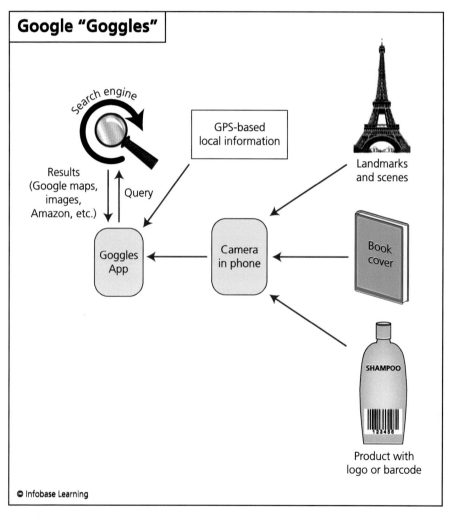

One of the most interesting search developments is the ability to capture images from cameras in mobile devices and feed them to search engines. As a result, users can obtain detailed information about a variety of places or objects simply by viewing them.

Page and Brin have incorporated their interest in alternative energy and transportation into various Google projects. In 2006, Page gave the keynote address in front of the VW Touareg Stanley robotic car at the Consumer Electronics Show in Las Vegas, Nevada. *(Barry Sweet/ZUMA Press/Newscom)*

## GOOGLING THE GENOME

While Google might in some ways be becoming more of a normal business, the data mining and artificial intelligence algorithms that have made Google so effective almost beg to be extended into new areas. One of these areas is health care, where one application involves the human genome, the database of instructions in DNA that determine much of the structure and characteristics of organisms, including human beings.

For Brin, the possibility of using advanced techniques to analyze the human genome has a personal dimension as well. Shortly before Brin's marriage, he learned that his mother had Parkinson's disease, a degenerative disorder of the central nervous system. As the disease progresses, patients experience tremors, rigidity, or difficulty in movement. Later, some patients experience problems with thinking and behavior, and even dementia. There is no cure for the disease, although drugs can help reduce the severity of the earliest symptoms.

Will we Google our genes someday? Sergey Brin and his wife Anne Wojcicki attend a party for the genetic research service 23andMe in New York City, 2008. *(Donald Bowers/Getty Images for the Weinstein Company)*

Page and Brin's wives share a strong interest in genetics. They founded a company called 23andMe (23 is the number of gene-carrying chromosomes in human beings). The purpose of the company is to create an affordable way for people to obtain a profile of their DNA. Many diseases, including Parkinson's, are more likely to occur when certain genes or combinations of genes are present.

In a 2008 Google conference, Brin announced that he is carrying a genetic mutation that increases the chance that he too will eventually develop Parkinson's disease. Since the disease typically does not arise until middle age, Brin noted in his personal blog that

> I feel fortunate to be in this position. Until the fountain of youth is discovered, all of us will have some conditions in our old age, only we don't know what they will be. I have a better guess than almost anyone else what ills may be mine—and I have decades to prepare for it.

In December 2008, Sergey and Anne Brin had their first child, a boy named Benji. He too might carry the mutation (if known, this information has been kept private). The following March Brin announced that Google would make a major donation to fund research on the genetics of Parkinson's disease to be done by 23andMe. The study hopes to identify other genes that might enable a more accurate prediction of whether someone will get Parkinson's.

Brin donated his own DNA to the study. He told *New York Times* reporter Andrew Pollack that

> I kind of give myself 50-50 odds of getting Parkinson's in 20 or so years, 25 years. But I also give it a 50-50 shot of medicine catching up to be able to deal with it.

Brin and Google see themselves as being in a unique position to aid in this effort.

Googlers seem to love a challenge even outside of work. Here, Google software engineer Amanda Camp is using the climbing wall at Google's Kirkland, Washington, office. *(Stephen Brashear/Getty Images)*

# THE ULTIMATE GOOGLE

Even as Google has grown from a cramped garage to a worldwide complex of data centers and laboratories, Page and Brin have remained remarkably consistent in their belief that a brighter future will be powered by people who are empowered by having access to all the world's information. Speaking to Search Engine Watch in 2003, Page's vision was that

> Artificial intelligence would be the ultimate version of Google. . . . It would understand exactly what you wanted, and it would give you the right thing. That's obviously artificial intelligence, to be able to answer any question, basically because almost everything is on the Web, right? We're nowhere near doing that now. However we can get. . . . closer to that, and that's basically what we're working on.

But if the day comes when Google can answer any question, what questions might we still be asking?

As quoted by Daniel Alef, Ken Auletta, in a discussion on the *Charlie Rose* television show, remarked, "Larry and Sergey are idealistic people. What happens ten years [down the road] if they're not there, the next generation?" After all, the generation that will shape what Google and the other major players of the Web will become has grown up in an already googlized world. As Brin told a group of Israeli high school students in 2003

> Two kind of crazy kids have had a big impact on the world because of the power of the Internet, the power of the distribution, and the power of software and computers. And there are so many things like that out there. There are so many opportunities where you can have a huge impact on the world by using the leverage of science and technology. All of you are uniquely positioned, and you should be excited about that

In the years since Brin spoke these words, there seems to have been no shortage of "crazy kids" bringing bold new ideas to technology. One need only think of Facebook and Twitter, or the endless new applications being found for smartphones. As Page said in comments in the October 2011 earnings announcement: ". . . we are still at the very early stages of what technology can deliver . . . these tools we use online will look very different in 5 years time." It is a safe bet that each new development will bring a new set of challenges and concerns.

# Chronology

**March 26, 1973**
Larry Page is born in East Lansing, Michigan

**August 31, 1973**
Sergey Brin is born in Moscow, capital of what was then the Soviet Union

**1975–1979**
Page attends the Okemos Montessori School

**1978**
The Brin family applies for emigration from the Soviet Union

**1979**
The Brins are allowed to emigrate; they arrive in the United States after spending some months in Paris

**1982**
Young Brin gets his first computer—a Commodore 64

**1989**
Brin graduates from high school and takes courses at the University of Maryland

**1990**
Tim Berners-Lee introduces the World Wide Web

**1991**
Page graduates from East Lansing High School

**1993**
Marc Andreesen and Eric Bina introduce Mosaic, the first graphical Web browser and predecessor of Netscape. The number of Web users begins to grow rapidly

**1994**
Brin graduates from the University of Maryland

**1995**
Page graduates from the University of Michigan; earns a B.S. in computer engineering

**1995**
Page and Brin meet at Stanford University; Microsoft CEO Bill Gates writes a memo saying that their company faced a new challenge from an "Internet tidal wave"

**1996**
Page and Brin begin to collaborate on a search engine called BackRub

**1997**
Page and Brin find a new name for their search engine—Google
They register the domain google.com

**August 1998**
Sun cofounder Andy von Bechtolsheim invests $100,000 as Google, Inc. is founded

**September 1998**
Google is formally incorporated and sets up its first headquarters in a garage in Menlo Park, California; Google hires its first employee, Craig Silverstein

**December 1998**
*PC Magazine* praises the quality of Google's search engine, naming it one of their top 100 Web sites for 1998; Google has now indexed about 60 million Web pages

**March 1999**
Too big for the garage, Google moves to offices in Palo Alto, now having eight employees

**June 1999**
Google receives $25 million from venture capitalists Sequoia Capital and Kleiner Perkins

**August 1999**
Google moves its corporate headquarters again, to Mountain View

**December 1999**
During CableFest, Google frantically tries to put together enough machines to serve a growing number of online searches

**January 2000**
Google launches the first version of AdWords

**March 2000**
Google launches its affiliate program; Page establishes a product review process

**April 1, 2000**
An April Fool's tradition is begun with the announcement of MentalPlex mind-reading search engine

**May 2000**
Google works furiously to accommodate Yahoo users while building a billion-address Web index; Google wins its first Webby award for technical achievement (according to judges) and Peoples' Voice (chosen by users)

**June 2000**
Google becomes Yahoo's default search engine, replacing Inktomi; Google's web index now includes 1 billion addresses

**December 2000**
Google offers its first toolbar, integrating its services directly into Web browsers

**March 2001**
Eric Schmidt becomes chairman of Google's board of directors; China blocks access to Google for the first time

**July 2001**
Google launches Image Search, with access to 250 million images

**August 2001**
Google opens its first international office, in Tokyo; Eric Schmidt becomes Google's CEO, with Page becoming president of products and Brin president of technology

**September 2001**
Google puts together improvised news and communications services in response to the September 11 terrorist attacks

**December 2001**
Google now indexes 3 billion Web addresses

**February 2002**
Google wins Earthlink's advertising business from Overture

**April 2002**
Google allows ad buyers to bid for AdWords; Overture sues Google, claiming patent violations; Google provides a set of functions allowing outside programs to use Google search facilities

**May 2002**
Google partners with America Online, allowing AOL and Compuserve users to use Google searches

**September 2002**
Google News launches with 4,000 news sources

**December 2002**
Froogle (later called Google Product Search) allows users to find, compare, and buy products

**February 2003**
Google buys blogger.com, an easy-to-use service for online personal postings

**March 2003**
New acquisitions help Google match Web sites to targeted ads

**June 2003**
Google launches AdSense, allowing advertisers to bid for ads targeted to Web content

**August 2003**
Google's revised browser toolbar includes a popup ad blocker and the ability to help users fill out forms

**October 2003**
Microsoft approaches Google about a possible merger or partnership, but nothing comes of it

**December 2003**
Google launches Google Print, which eventually develops into the massive and controversial project to scan and index the world's books

**January 2004**
Google's Orkut marks its first venture into social networking

**February 2004**
Larry Page is inducted into the National Academy of Engineering; Google's Web index hits 6 billion items, including 880 million images

**March 2004**
Google moves to a larger world headquarters or Googleplex in Mountain View. The company now has 800 employees; Google introduces Google Local, customizing search results for a given area

**April 2004**
Google files papers for its initial public offering; Google launches Gmail, a Web-based email service. Automatic matching of ads to e-mail content creates controversy

**August 19, 2004**
Google's initial public offering (IPO) of 19,605,052 shares takes place on Wall Street. The initial share price is $85 but rises to $100 by day's end

**October 2004**
Page and Brin are named fellows of the Marconi Society, honoring their contribution to communications science and the Internet; Google introduces Desktop Search, enlisting the search engine to help users find files on their PCs

**November 2004**
Google now indexes 8 billion items on the Web

**December 2004**
Google makes book scanning agreements with libraries at Harvard, Stanford, the University of Michigan, Oxford, and the New York Public Library—more will follow

**February 2005**
Google Maps is introduced

**June 2005**
Google inaugurates Summer of Code, a project engaging computer science students in creative and challenging software projects; Google introduces a version of its search facilities formatted for smartphones and other mobile devices; Google Earth combines satellite imagery with images of buildings and terrain

**September–October 2005**
In separate lawsuits, the Authors Guild and the Association of American Publishers charge Google with violating copyright law by digitizing books without permission of copyright holders

**November 2005**
Google Print is renamed Google Book Search; Google Analytics offers Web site owners detailed information about how their site is being accessed

**June 2006**
Google acquires and revamps Picasa, an online photo sharing service

**September 2006**
Google begins philanthropic grants through Google.org and the Google Foundation, directed by Larry Brilliant

**October 2006**
Google acquires YouTube

**May 2007**
Google introduces Street View to Google Maps, starting with five U.S. cities; Brin marries Anne Wojcicki

**June 2007**
Google announces a variety of green initiatives, including installation of solar panels at the Googleplex and a program to reduce the environmental impact of computer use

**August 2007**
Google Earth adds views of the sky and the universe beyond

**September 2007**
Continuing its cosmic outreach, Google and the X PRIZE Foundation announce a contest to build an exploration robot and send it to the Moon

**November 2007**
Google announces Android, an operating system for cell phones and other mobile devices; Page marries Lucy Southworth

**December 2007**
Google announces RE<C, an initiative to develop clean energy technologies worldwide

**February 2008**
Acquiring and revamping the JotSpot service, Google introduces Google Sites, providing Wiki-like tools for creating collaborative Web sites

**May 2008**
Google Health provides a way for users to store and manage their medical records

**July 2008**
The total number of Web addresses indexed by Google reaches 1 trillion

**September 2008**
Google introduces the Chrome web browser; Google celebrates its 10th anniversary

**October 2008**
Google agrees to pay $125 million to authors and publishers to compensate for copyright violations—a system for sharing future revenues is also set up

**November 2008**
Google uses search trends to track flu epidemics faster than with traditional methods

**February 2009**
Google Earth adds detailed coverage of the ocean floor

**March 2009**
Google Voices integrates the ability to make Internet-based phone calls with Gmail

**June 2009**
Microsoft rebrands its live search as Bing. The improved search engine makes modest headway against the dominant Google

**October 2009**
Further integration with social networks: Twitter updates are now included in search results and the experimental Social Search lets users keep track of their friends' contact information and postings

**November 2009**
Google opens Chromium, an open source operating system

**December 2009**
Google begins to provide search results customized for each user

**January 2010**
The first Google-branded smartphone, the Nexus One, is introduced; Google announces that it will no longer directly censor search results in China—users are redirected to an uncensored site based in Hong Kong

**April 2010**
Left out of earlier cases, visual artists such as photographers sue Google over its online display and indexing of their images

**May 2010**
Google reveals that its Street View program had collected data transmitted over unencrypted wifi networks. The company insisted the data collection was inadvertent, but it lead to investigations by U.S. and European regulators;

The Google TV service is announced, providing users with easy access to information about and content of TV shows and movies

**June 2010**
Faced with the likelihood its Chinese operating license would not be renewed, Google changes its mainland site so that it does not automatically redirect users to Hong Kong

**July 2010**
Google announces a personalized version of its news service

**August 2010**
A U.S. district court rules that Google did not harm the company Rosetta Stone by using its trademark as an AdSense trigger

**November 2010**
The European Commission announces that it is investigating Google for allegedly preferring its own services in Web search results while downgrading its rating of others

**December 2010**
Google introduces a pilot program to distribute notebook computers running Chrome OS, its new Web-based cloud operating system; Google launches Google eBooks, offering electronic versions of books that can be read online or downloaded

**January 2011**
Google's speak to Tweet service allows people who have phones but no Internet access to create Twitter posts—the micro-blogging service allows people involved in uprisings in Egypt and elsewhere a way to get around government censorship and Internet blocks

**March 2011**
A federal judge rejects the settlement of the lawsuits involving Google Books; Microsoft sues Google in European Union court, claiming that the latter has a monopoly in the search market

**April 2011**
Larry Page takes over as Google's CEO; Google invests $168 million in a solar power plant in California's Mojave Desert and $100 million in a wind power farm

**June 2011**
Google announces Google+, a social networking service expected to compete with Facebook

**July 2011**
Google reportedly faces antitrust probes by both the Federal Trade Commission and the U.S. Senate; As Google announces record earnings, Page says that the company will concentrate on core projects and announces that Google Labs, source of many innovations, will be closed

**August 2011**
Google announces its intent to acquire Motorola Mobility, strengthening its position in the patent wars over Android

**September 2011**
Google+ is opened to the public and gains more than 40 million users

**October 2011**
Google announces a strong third quarter, with revenue up 33 percent from the preceding year; Google steps up the pace of acquisition, buying restaurant reviewer Zagat for $151 million; Microsoft and Google are reported to be interested in making major investments in Yahoo in order to tap into its still large user base

**February 2012**
French regulators express strong concerns about Google's combining user data collected under many separate services. They unsuccessfully urge Google to delay adoption of new privacy policies. Meanwhile U.S. lawmakers and regulators express similar concerns.

**March 2012**
Google's new privacy policy and terms of service consolidate what had been more than 60 separate policies into a simpler, easier to read text. Google will also provide more tools to help users see what information is being collected and to control how it is used.

**April 2012**
Google announces strong revenues of $10.65 billion for the first quarter of 2012, with Page saying that "We are still at the very early stages of what technology can do to improve peoples' lives." The dispute over whether Google's Android operating system violates Oracle's copyrights in its use of the Java programming language reaches court.

# Glossary

**adSense**   a program through which Web site owners agree with Google to have ads appear on their sites, mainly based on their site's content. Advertisers bid for placement and Google and site owners share the advertising fees based on the number of times the ad is shown or clicked on.

**AdWords**   a Google program where advertisers could pay to have their text ads appear in search results, based on selected keywords. A feature where advertisers bid on keywords was added later.

**affiliate program**   any program where a Web site pays other sites to send it business via a link. Amazon has made such arrangements to promote books; Google has done it by having sites embed special search boxes.

**algorithm**   a procedure for solving a problem or performing some other task, embodied in computer programming code.

**America Online (AOL)**   an online service that began in the days of dial-up connections. It introduced millions of people to online chat, games, and shopping, but has had difficulty adapting to the modern Web.

**Android**   Google's operating system primarily used for smartphones and tablet computers.

**app**   a relatively small program that provides features for another platform such as a mobile device or web browser.

**backlink**   a link from a Web page back to the page that referred to it.

**banner ad**   an ad or group of ads that appear across the top of a Web page.

**beta test**   the testing of software that is functional but not yet bug-free and perhaps not complete. Often people are invited to participate or a certain number of volunteers are accepted.

**Chrome**   Google's streamlined entry into the Web browser market, competing with Microsoft's Internet Explorer, Mozilla Firefox, and other browsers.

**Chrome OS**   Google's Web-based operating system. All user interaction is through a version of the Chrome browser, and user data is stored on Google's servers.

**clickthrough rate (CTR)**   The percentage of people who see an ad who click on it to go to the advertiser's site. Generally the better the ad is targeted to be relevant to consumers, the higher the clickthrough rate.

**cloud computing**   The growing trend to provide both applications and data storage from online servers, rather than storing them on a traditional PC.

**computer science**   The study of the principles behind the storage and processing of information in computers.

**cookie**   a file that a Web site stores on the user's computer in order to be able to identify the user and retrieve a profile, allowing for targeted advertising, maintenance of shopping carts, customization of the user interface, and other features.

**cyberbullying**   severe or repeated ridicule, intimidation or harassment using online services.

**database**   any organized collection of information that can be searched or processed systematically.

**data mining**   the automatic extraction and analysis of patterns and relationships within a mass of data, such as customer transactions.

**disintermediation**   the removing of the middleman in a transaction, such as an artist selling music directly to consumers rather than through a record label.

**dot-com**   an Internet-based business (named from the .com in Web addresses).

**dot-com bubble**   the collapse in stock prices for many of the first Internet-based companies, in the early 2000s.

**e-book**   a book whose text is distributed electronically rather than in printed form.

**e-commerce**   selling of goods or services through Web sites.

**e-reader**   a handheld device for reading e-books and other text.

**Facebook**   the world's most popular social networking site. Users create profiles and share updates with their network of friends.

**filter bubble**   the situation in which customized online content is selected and presented according to a profile of the user's interests.

**google**   as a verb, to search for something on the Web.

**google bombing**   manipulating Google's index by placement of keywords in anchor text, sometimes linking unflattering search phrases to certain companies or presidential candidates.

**Google Docs**   Google's Web-based ("cloud") office suite, providing word processing, spreadsheet, and other functions.

**Googleplex**   Google's name for its world corporate headquarters in Menlo Park, California, which is a large campus with dozens of buildings.

**Google+ (plus)**   the latest entry by Google into social networking, competing with Facebook.

**GoTo**   Later named Overture, this company came up with the idea of having advertisers bid on ad placements based on search terms. The company was later bought by Yahoo! and a legal settlement allowed Google to use this advertising method in its AdWords program.

**GPS (global positioning system)**   a satellite-based system that can pinpoint the location of a device to within a few yards.

**HTML (hypertext markup language)**   a method for formatting text and other elements of Web pages, including links to other pages.

**HTTP (hypertext transmission protocol)**   a set of procedures that allows information to be exchanged between Web servers, browsers, and other programs.

**incremental index**   an index that is being continually updated as the latest findings are integrated into the main index.

**index**   the database relating search words and phrases to the addresses of Web pages containing them.

**initial public offering (IPO)**   the first time a company offers shares of its stock to the public.

**intellectual property**   creative work (such as books, music, or inventions) that is protected by law.

**Internet**   a worldwide network connecting computers and related devices to exchange information by following agreed formats and procedures.

**Internet Service Provider (ISP)**   a company that provides a connection to the Internet. They can also host (provide space for) Web sites.

**keyword**   a word or phrase that identifies what someone is trying to find online.

**long tail**   in retailing, the idea that it can be profitable to serve many individuals or small markets if the costs of processing and distribution are low.

**mashup**   a web page or application that combines data or functions from separate programs into a new display.

**monetize**  to find a way to make money from an activity, such as Web searching.

**netbook**  a small laptop computer used mainly for Web surfing, email, and other light applications.

**network effect**  the growth in value of a service as it gains users, thus making it more attractive and shutting out competitors.

**open source**  program code that is freely available for anyone to use, modify, and distribute.

**PageRank**  an algorithm based on evaluating the number and quality of links to a Web page, in order to prioritize search results. (The "Page" part can be read to refer either to "Web page" or "Larry Page.").

**pay per click (PPC)**  an amount paid by an advertiser each time a user clicks on a Web ad.

**query**  a search of the Web or a database.

**scale up**  to expand smoothly and economically in response to increased demands or requirements.

**search engine**  software that retrieves Web sites related to keywords entered by the user.

**search engine optimization (SEO)**  services offered by companies that claim to be able to influence how high a business appears in a Google search results list. The effectiveness of such techniques is controversial.

**server**  A computer or group of computers that provides information or services to users. Also, the software that runs on such machines.

**smartphone**  a cell phone capable of Internet access, email, and running applications (apps).

**spam**  mass-distributed email offering dubious products or services, and often used to spread viruses and other forms of malware.

**spider**  *see* WEB CRAWLER.

**start-up**  a new company that has just begun operations and may still be developing its first product.

**streaming**  delivery of sound or video files on demand from a server. By loading an initial portion into a buffer area, the content can be listened to or watched with minimal interruption.

**tablet**  a slatelike computer such as the Apple iPad, running small programs called apps.

**targeting**  setting up ads so they are displayed (served) under certain conditions, such as the presence of a keyword in a search or in the text of a Web page.

**20 percent time**   the Google policy of encouraging Google engineers to spend one day a week developing ideas not related to their primary assignment.

**Twitter**   an immensely popular "micro-blogging" site where users can post short text updates and keep track of one another's activities.

**URL (Uniform Resource Locator)**   the unique address identifying a page on the Web. For example Google's home page is www.google.com.

**user interface (UI)**   the aspects of a software program or Web page through which users interact with the service. Elements of a UI might include menus, search boxes, check boxes, lists, etc.

**venture capitalist**   an investor who seeks promising startup companies and provides them with money in exchange for a stake in the business.

**Web browser**   one of a variety of programs that allows users to retrieve and display Web pages.

**Web crawler (or spider)**   software that systematically follows Web links and indexes sites for later retrieval by a search engine.

**Web portal**   A site that presents selected Web links organized by topic for easy browsing. (A portal may also offer a search engine.)

**Web server**   software that accepts Web connection requests and provides the requested pages or other resources.

**Wi-Fi**   a widely used radio system for connecting portable computers, cell phones, and other devices to Internet access points.

**World Wide Web**   a vast system allowing pages of information and other resources to be linked together over the Internet.

**Yahoo**   the largest and most successful Web portal.

# Further Resources

## Books

Auletta, Ken. *Googled: The End of the World as We Know It.* New York: Penguin Press, 2009.

*Despite the rather bombastic title, this is a detailed and balanced history of Google, much of it told through quotations from top Google executives and outside commentators and critics.*

Battelle, John. *The Search.* New York: Portfolio, 2005.

*An experienced observer of the computer industry offers a book that focuses not on the history of Google as such, but the history of an idea—Web search—and how it played out in the hands of Google and others.*

Brandt, Richard. *Inside Larry and Sergey's Brain.* New York: Portfolio, 2009.

*A biography of Larry Page and Sergey Brin that focuses on how they tackled particular projects such as the ambitious effort to digitize the world's books.*

Cleland, Scott, with Ira Brodsky. *Search & Destroy: Why You Can't Trust Google, Inc.* St. Louis, Mo.: Telescope Books, 2011.

*A somewhat tendentious and repetitive account of the dangers posed by Google's information practices. However, it does raise some important issues.*

Girard, Bernard. *The Google Way: How One Company Is Revolutionizing Management as We Know It.* San Francisco, Calif.: No Starch Press, 2009.

*Analyzes Google's rise and practices from a business theory point of view. Identifies the key principles of Google's management and business plan.*

Levy, Steven. *In the Plex: How Google Thinks, Works and Shapes Our Lives.* New York: Simon & Schuster, 2011.

*A long-time writer about the culture of computing tackles Google, observing "Googlers" at work and play, recounting Google's corporate culture, and delving into the personalities of Larry Page, Sergey Brin, Eric Schmidt, and others.*

Lowe, Janet. *Google Speaks: Secrets of the World's Greatest Billionaire Entrepreneurs, Sergey Brin and Larry Page.* Hoboken, N.J.: Wiley, 2009.

*A lively, conversational look at Page, Brin, the development of Google, its business strategies, and the controversies surrounding some of the company's practices.*

McPherson, Stephanie Sammartino. *Sergey Brin and Larry Page: Founders of Google.* (USA Lifeline Biographies). Minneapolis, Minn.: Twenty-First Century Books, 2010.

*A biography supplemented by a number of original news features from USA Today.*

Pariser, Eli. *The Filter Bubble: What the Internet Is Hiding from You.* New York: Penguin Press, 2011.

*A detailed argument about how online companies such as Google are shaping the kind of news and other information people receive online. The trend toward personalization or customization can result in people only receiving content that reinforces their existing views.*

Stross, Randall E. *Planet Google: One Company's Audacious Plan to Organize Everything We Know.* New York: Free Press, 2008.

*A business professor provides a detailed but quite readable account of Google's founding and development, including its technical prowess and business model.*

Vaidhyanathan, Siva. *The Googlization of Everything (And Why We Should Worry).* Berkeley: University of California Press, 2011.

*A critical look at the influence of Google that argues that its services influence public perception and access to information in many subtle ways, while lacking transparency as to its procedures and agenda.*

Vise, David, and Mark Malseed. *The Google Story.* Updated ed. New York: Delacorte, 2008.

*Updated for Google's 10th anniversary, one of the best accounts of Page, Brin, and Schmidt. Includes much original material from interviews with Google employees and others.*

## Web Resources

American Academy of Achievement. "Larry Page Interview." Available online. URL: http://www.achievement.org/autodoc/page/pag0int-1. Accessed June 4, 2011.

*Page and Brin talk about their childhood and how they became interested in science and computers.*

Archive of Google Home Pages, 1997–2011. Available online. URL: http://blogoscoped.com/archive/2006-04-21-n63.html. Accessed October 28, 2011.

*A collection showing how Google's home page has changed over the years, while retaining an essential simplicity.*

Battelle, John. "The Birth of Google." *Wired* (August 2005). Available online. URL: http://www.wired.com/wired/archive/13.08/battelle.html. Accessed October 28, 2011.

*Recounts how Page's and Brin's obsession with Web links led to the creation of Google.*

Brin, Sergey. "A Library to Last Forever." *New York Times* (October 8, 2009). Available online. URL: http://www.nytimes.com/2009/10/09/opinion/09brin.html. Accessed October 28, 2011.

*In this op-ed piece, Brin talks about how valuable knowledge is rapidly lost as books go out of print, and how he and Page have struggled to create a digital library that could preserve knowledge indefinitely and make it much more accessible to researchers. He defends the legal settlement and argues that author and publisher rights will be adequately protected.*

"Eric Schmidt, Larry Page, Sergey Brin at Zeitgeist Europe 08." Available online. URL: http://www.youtube.com/watch?v=1acoC5zjgM0. Accessed October 28, 2011.

*Video of interviews with the Google founders and then-CEO Schmidt at Google's Zeitgeist Conference, 2008.*

Google Corporate Information. Available online. URL: http://www.google.com/intl/en/about/corporate/. Accessed October 28, 2011.

*Google describes its corporate mission, culture, principles, and philosophy.*

Google Founders' Letters. Available online. URL: http://investor.google.com/corporate/founders-letter.html. Accessed October 28, 2011.

*Since 2004, Page and Brin have taken turns writing these letters to Google's stockholders, recounting their achievements of the past year and vision for the future.*

Heilemann, John. "The History of Internet Search and Google." Discovery Science. YouTube. Available online. URL: http://www.youtube.com/watch?v=iBCSibI4ffg&feature=related. Accessed October 28, 2011.

*A documentary that introduces the Internet players of the late 1990s and early 2000s and explains how Google redefined not only Web search but also the whole online experience.*

"Larry Page, Sergey Brin and Larry Brilliant." Global Philanthropy Forum. Fora TV. Available online. URL: http://fora.tv/2007/04/11/Larry_Page_Sergey_Brin_and_Larry_Brilliant. Accessed October 28, 2011.

*Video of a conference in which the Google founders and Google Foundation director Larry Brilliant discuss the ideas behind and goals of Google's philanthropic efforts.*

"Larry Page's University of Michigan Commencement Address." Google.com. URL: http://www.google.com/intl/en/press/annc/20090502-page-commencement.html. Accessed October 28, 2011.

*Transcript of Page's 2009 address to graduating University of Michigan students.*

"Life at Google: Organizational Culture." eCorner (Stanford University's Entrepreneurship Corner). May 1, 2002. Available online. URL: http://ecorner.stanford.edu/authorMaterialInfo.html?mid=1072. Accessed October 28, 2011.

*Videos of a talk about life, work, and research at Google, just after it signed its big contract with AOL.*

Official Google Blog. Available online. URL: http://googleblog.blogspot.com/. Accessed October 28, 2011.

*Google developers and others talk about the latest Google products, as well as life and work at Google.*

Pew Internet and American Life Project. Available online. URL: http://pewinternet.org/. Accessed October 28, 2011.

*A respected long-term research project that surveys and analyzes peoples' online behavior, including use of search engines and other services.*

Search Engine Land. Available online. URL: http://searchengineland.com/. Accessed October 28, 2011.

*An excellent source of news and commentary about search engines, online advertising, marketing, and related issues.*

"Sergey Brin & Larry Page: Larry Page Interview." Academy of Achievement (October 28, 2000). Available online. URL: http://www.achievement.org/autodoc/page/pag0int-1. Accessed October 28, 2011.

*The two Google founders talk about their childhood interests, what has motivated them to create their search engine and other products, and their ultimate vision for the future.*

Stone, Brad. "Larry Page's Google 3.0." Bloomberg Businessweek. Available online. URL: http://www.businessweek.com/magazine/content/11_06/b4214050441614.htm. Accessed October 28, 2011.
*Describes how Larry Page, moving into Google's CEO slot, is likely to change the course of a company that may have become too large and bureaucratic.*

Suarez, Paul. "Best of Google Labs: A Retrospective." CIO.com Available online. URL: http://www.cio.com/article/686589/Best_of_Google_Labs_A_Retrospective. Accessed October 28, 2011.
*Slide shows and articles about Google labs and other Google innovations.*

Sullivan, Danny. "Google's Facebook Competitor, The Google+ Social Network, Finally Arrives." Search Engine Land (June 28, 2011). Available online. URL: http://searchengineland.com/googles-facebook-competitor-the-google-social-network-finally-arr ives-83401. Accessed October 28, 2011.
*Describes and evaluates Google's latest foray into social networking and looks at its prospects for making inroads against Facebook.*

Temple, James. "Google's Larry Page Must Mend Image of Firm, Self." SFGate in *San Francisco Chronicle* (April 3, 2011). Available online. URL: http://www.sfgate.com/cgi-bin/article.cgi?f=/c/a/2011/04/03/BU4Q1IMF52.DTL. Accessed October 28, 2011.
*Newly installed as CEO, Larry Page faces many challenges. Perhaps the most important is that of repairing the public image of Google, and Page's temperament may not be suited to the task.*

What Do You Love? Available online. URL: http://www.wdyl.com. Accessed October 28, 2011.
*An experimental Google Web site that takes a search word or phrase and shows how a variety of Google products can enable the searcher to get more information about it or share information with others.*

"Why Google Won Desktop Search." eCorner (Stanford University's Entrepreneurship Corner). (October 7, 2010). Available online. URL: http://ecorner.stanford.edu/authorMaterialInfo.html?mid=2510 Accessed October 28, 2011.
*Dan Rosensweig, former COO of Yahoo, explains how Google won the battle for the desktop search market during the mid-2000s. While Yahoo was*

*an expansive Web portal that tried to provide many kinds of services, Google focused on search, offered users the most useful results, and then leveraged this tool into relationships with many Web sites.*

Wiggins, Richard W. "The Effects of September 11 on the Leading Search Engine." *First Monday* 6, no. 10 (October 1, 2001). Available online. URL: http://firstmonday.org/htbin/cgiwrap/bin/ojs/index.php/fm/article/view/890/799. Accessed October 28, 2011.

*Analyzes how Internet users sought information following the terrorist attacks of September 11, 2001, the role played by Google as the leading search provider, and Google's evolution as a news provider.*

Zorpette, Glenn, and John Rennie. "Super Socialize Me: The Social Era of the Web Starts Now." *IEEE Spectrum* (June 2011). Available online. URL: http://spectrum.ieee.org/static/special-report-the-social-web. Accessed October 28, 2011.

*Reports on the importance of social networking for the future of the Web and the growing battle between Google and Facebook.*

# Index

Page numbers followed by *f* indicate
figures and images.

## A

Ackerman, Elise, 79
AdSense program, 38
advertising
    by AOL, 33–34
    by Google, 35–38
        effectiveness of, 37–38
        in Gmail, 55, 56
        innovations in, xvi, 34, 37–38
        in local search, 46–47
        marketers v. engineers in, 35–36
        origins of, 33
        personalization filters and, 96
        revenue from, 38
        social aspects of, 29, 78
        on YouTube, 69
    in journalism, 64
    by Yahoo, 29
AdWords program, 34, 37–38
Alef, Daniel, 54, 92, 106
algorithms. *See also* PageRank
    in advertising, 38
    definition of, 16
    gaming of, 39
    in personalization filters, 96
Allen, Paul, 51
Altavista search engine, 14, 16
alternative energy, 4, 81, 103f
Amazon.com, 11, 54, 60, 61, 94
America Online, 33–34, 93
Analytics, Google, 38
Anderson, Sean, 19
Android operating system, 69–72
    in Google TV, 68
    patent challenges to, 72, 100

    structure of, 71f
    users of, 69–70
antitrust complaints, 100
AOL, 33–34, 93
Apple Computer
    iOS of, 69, 70
    mobile devices of, 70, 87
    in patent disputes, 72
    Schmidt at, 40
    television service of, 68
apps, 69
Arab Spring, 84
arrogance, 41, 101
artificial intelligence, 106
Asia
    censorship in, 82–84, 83f
    Internet users in, 82, 85f
Auletta, Ken, 4, 44, 54, 61, 67, 69, 70, 89–91,
    94–95, 106
Australia, Street View in, 50, 51
authors, and Google Books, 53
Ayers, Charlie, 30

## B

backlinks, 16
BackRub, 15–16, 18–19
Baidu search engine, 84
banner ads, 37
BASIC language, 7
Battelle, John, 5, 9, 11–12, 23, 43
Bauer, John, 34
Bechtolsheim, Andy von, 23–24
Berners-Lee, Tim, 10, 12–13
beta tests, 54, 77
Bezos, Jeff, 60
Bill & Melinda Gates Foundation, 80–81
Bing search engine, market share of, xv
bombing, google, 39